A Curious Cook: Life Beyond the "Free From" Aisle

A vegetarian field guide for coeliacs

Bridget Morton

Clink Street

London | New York

Published by Clink Street Publishing 2021

Copyright © 2021

First edition.

ISBN:
978-1-912850-23-5 - hardback
978-1-912850-24-2 - ebook

To Roy for all his support – and the veg

And Joan whose idea this book was – take it up with her

List of Contents

Introduction

So, you have been diagnosed with coeliac disease and everything is awful and dreadful and life isn't fair. Well, yes. And then again, no. Alright, you're fed up that you have to check every label very carefully unlike your non-coeliac friends and family who reach so carelessly for that lovely sourdough loaf (okay, that bit really isn't fair). But you now have an opportunity to explore culinary highways and byways you would not otherwise have gone down. A whole new world of lovely food awaits you. No, it's not the *same* food, but it is just as delicious.

If you are excluding gluten from your diet because you think it makes you feel better but don't have any sort of diagnosis, please do seek medical advice. It may just be masking another condition which should be treated.

You can over-complicate cooking. Freshly foraged larks' breath served on a bed of pretension, which takes twenty chefs using tweezers to assemble, is all very fine and large for expensive and exclusive restaurants, but mere mortals want food that is nourishing, comforting, and above all enjoyable to prepare and to eat. When I was first diagnosed with coeliac disease I was determined that I wasn't going to be exiled to the supermarket 'free from' aisle, full of unappetising packages of expensive food which looks and tastes like cardboard. To misquote that well known philosopher and bon viveur Crocodile Dundee, you can eat it (just about) but you wouldn't want to live on it.

I bought a couple of recipe books. They encouraged me to buy a plethora of flours and use them in a rainbow of combinations, and none of it quite worked. Maybe it was because the writers were not coeliacs. They don't have to cook and eat these recipes on a daily or weekly basis, and indeed store twelve different kinds of flour in their kitchen. Time to simplify. After a little experimentation I settled on using four flours: brown rice, chickpea, polenta and tapioca. There's a lot you can do with these simple ingredients.

I would encourage you to use local independent shops where you can. You build up a relationship with the shop owners. They will often order things specifically for you or, if you buy something in bulk quantities, reduce the price. The wonderful Il Principe on the Cowley Road where we buy Barilla gluten free pasta (the best brand I have come across) knocks 10% off when we order a whole box at a time. That's ten to twelve packets depending on the type of pasta. You need somewhere to store it of course, but if you can, it makes it more affordable.

It is actually quite hard to produce inedible cooking, even if you make a mistake, unless that mistake is adding 200 g of salt to a cake mix thinking that it's sugar. Most mistakes teach you something, like not to make them again, but also about flavour and texture. I think what I am saying is, as Douglas Adams put it in *The Hitchhiker's Guide to the Galaxy*, don't panic. If you don't like a particular ingredient, or can't get hold of it, substitute something else. Try doing the same dish but using a different vegetable, or pulse or fruit. There is no right and wrong unless you are doing classic French cooking, and we most definitely are not. Cooking should be fun, almost as much fun as eating.

I am not a vegetarian. So why are you writing a vegetarian cookbook I hear you ask. Good question. I *was* a vegetarian for about fifteen years. This was not because I think eating meat is wrong. We are omnivores. I see nothing morally problematic in eating meat as long as we do it ethically: good husbandry, eat meat in moderation, nose to tail eating. I became a vegetarian in the wake of the food scandals of the 1980s. You may well be too young to remember this, and many of those who were there at the time forget. It wasn't just Creutzfeldt-Jakob disease (CJD). It was the revelation that farmers were routinely adding growth promoters, including antibiotics, to animal feed. It was also the time of the domination of food shopping by big supermarkets, often out of town, and labelling was in its infancy. I had no idea what was in the meat I was buying, so I stopped buying it and became a vegetarian. Being in my early twenties when this happened meant that my formative years as a cook were also as a vegetarian. It is still my comfort zone. I do cook with meat but it tends to be in a supporting role to vegetables and pulses. I like meat, but I really can't eat a lot of it.

The second reason for writing a vegetarian cookbook is that I think if you are a meat eating coeliac, whilst there are problems, you can relatively easily construct a 'meat and two veg' meal avoiding gluten. If you are a vegetarian it is more problematic. Pastry dishes are a problem and also many recipes for what I will cautiously call burgers, include breadcrumbs. Fear not, there are alternatives.

Veganism is becoming very popular, and many of these recipes contain no dairy or egg. These are labelled with the code (Vg). Others could be adapted to suit vegans by substituting one or more ingredients with suitable alternatives. If you are a vegan who has recently been diagnosed with coeliac disease, or a coeliac who is considering becoming vegan, I would urge you to seek advice from a dietician or GP to ensure you are getting all the nutrients you need.

Conversion Tables

My partner Roy is a scientist by training so we live in a fully metricated house. Well, almost. We have a set of imperial weights, as well as the metric ones, which came with the second hand set of scales from the local market. Most measuring jugs come with both metric and imperial measures. But it's always helpful to have a ready reckoner.

Oven Temperatures

Gas Mark	°F	°C
1	275	140
2	300	150
3	235	170
4	350	180
5	375	190
6	400	200
7	425	220
8	450	230

Weights

Whilst researching conversion tables I discovered that they are not exact. In order to avoid having silly fractions in the measurements, they are approximate. It is important therefore that when following a recipe you do not mix metric and imperial measurements, but stick to one or the other.

½ oz	10 g
1 oz	25 g
2 oz	55 g
4 oz1	10 g
8 oz	210 g
1 lb	450 g
2 lbs	900 g

Volume

2 fl oz	55 ml
¼ pint (5 fl oz)	150 ml
½ pint	275 ml
1 pint	570 ml
1 ¾ pints	1 litre

The Basics

Store Cupboard Essentials

I'm not going to tell you what to keep in your store cupboard but I am going to tell you what is in mine for these dishes. Any dish can be made more luxurious by adding more expensive ingredients and many can be made less rich and more every day by using something which is good but cheaper.

Brown Rice Flour – this is a very dry flour and provides a good base for pastry and biscuits when mixed with the more absorbent gram and tapioca flours. Brown rice flour is more nutritious than white rice flour so try to get hold of it if you can. If you can't, use white rice flour instead.

Chickpea or Gram Flour – also known as besan. Gram flour is great for binding other ingredients together and is very nutritious. You always need to sieve it to get rid of the clumps.

Polenta – made from maize. It is sometimes sold as corn flour or corn grits. Coarse polenta makes a good substitute for breadcrumbs when coating rissoles etc. and fine polenta is also a useful ingredient in cakes and biscuits.

Tapioca Flour – this is made from the starch from cassava root and is not the same as cassava flour. It does not contain much nutrition but is absorbent and therefore useful in small quantities mixed with other flours to help retain moisture.

Xanthan Gum – this is a binding agent. It is produced when a sugar (glucose, sucrose or lactose) is fermented by the bacterium Xanthomonas campestris. Isopropyl alcohol is then added to make it a solid, after which it is dried and ground into a fine powder. It is actually an additive in many common foodstuffs as well as being used in the cosmetics industry. So although you may not have come across it when baking you will almost certainly have eaten it.

Glycerin – helps to retain moisture in cakes etc.

Tinned Chickpeas – invaluable for knocking up quick meals and for hummus, but **not** and I repeat **not**, for falafel.

Dried Chickpeas – for making falafel.

Feta Cheese (in the fridge) – keeps for ages and you can use it for tarts, salads and small pastries.

Halloumi Cheese (in the fridge) – keeps for ages and good for grilling, pizzette, tarts, etc.

Lemons and Limes – add sourness to all manner of dishes, great for dressing salads, the zest is wonderful in biscuits and cakes.

Sugar – now I should not be encouraging you to keep this, but you can't make puddings without it. You need icing sugar for pastry, demerara, muscovado and soft brown for cakes, puddings and biscuits. Try to use it sparingly.

Herbs and Spices – I mostly use fresh herbs which is easy for me because we grow them. Even if you only have a windowsill you can grow pots of herbs if you have sufficient light. It's cheaper than buying fresh herbs from a supermarket. If you cannot get hold of fresh then substitute dried ones. Be careful with amounts as the taste will be much stronger and don't store them for too long as the flavour will deteriorate.

I get spices from our wonderful Indian, Chinese and Middle Eastern shops on the Cowley Road, but supermarkets now stock a huge range. See the website section for sourcing more obscure ones.

Dough

So, keeping it simple I have one recipe for shortcrust pastry, one for sweet pastry and one for a basic flatbread which can be also be used to make samosas and other small pastries. The recipes for shortcrust pastry and flatbread can be found at the beginning of the next two chapters. The recipe for sweet crust pastry is at the beginning of the chapter called Sugar. This covers cakes, biscuits and puddings but let's be honest, it's about that sugar rush and it's not good for you.

I am a great believer in disaggregating tasks, breaking them down into simple steps which make the whole operation seem more achievable. All these doughs can be made ahead of time, kept in the fridge for twenty-four hours before using, and frozen. In fact the flatbread dough will keep in the fridge for up to a week. Make a double quantity and freeze half. Or make the pastry and cook the pastry case, leaving it to fill the next day.

Chapter 1

Savoury Tarts and Pies

Now, here's the thing, this pastry is your new best friend. It is easy to make, doesn't need to be rolled out – in fact don't even try, it will end in tears as you attempt to lift it into your pie dish and it falls into pieces. Because it has no gluten you can't overwork it, and as it cooks it firms and comes away from the pie dish so it's easy to cut and lift out. And best of all, provided you bake it blind you will never have a soggy bottom. Oh, and it tastes good. Just don't tell the others. Makes enough to line a standard flan case.

- *130 g brown rice flour*
- *30 g tapioca flour*
- *20 g gram flour*
- *90 g olive oil spread*
- *1 egg, beaten*
- *½ tsp xanthan gum*
- *Pinch of salt*

Sift the flours together in a bowl with the xanthan gum and salt. Rub in the olive oil spread until you have the texture of fine breadcrumbs. Beat the egg, and add gradually until the mixture comes together in a ball. Eggs differ in size, you may not need it all. If your mixture is a bit sticky just sift over a tablespoon of gram flower and mix in. You are now ready to deploy.

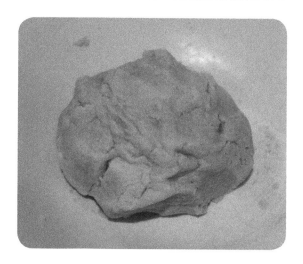

- 1 quantity of shortcrust pastry
- 280–300 g broad beans (podded weight)
- 200 g halloumi, grated
- 4 eggs
- 100 ml full cream milk
- 1 tsp dried oregano
- Pepper

If you grow your own broad beans this is a good recipe for a glut. If you don't grow your own and/or you think you don't like broad beans the secret is to peel the individual beans. Those that you buy in the supermarket will be older and tougher. Removing the outer skin reveals the tender bean inside. Yes, it sounds like a faff, but just turn on the radio and pour yourself a glass of wine. It's actually very therapeutic.

Preheat the oven to 180°C. Press the pastry into a standard 23 cm diameter flan dish, pushing the dough along the bottom and up the sides. You do not need to grease the dish: the pastry will come away cleanly from the sides as it cooks. Trim the top, prick the base all over with a fork, and line with baking parchment and baking beans. Cook for 10 minutes, turn oven down to 160°C, cook for another 10 minutes. Remove beans and cook for a further 5–10 minutes. Take out of the oven and turn the temperature up to 180°C.

Whilst the pastry is baking, put the beans in a saucepan with enough water to cover, bring to the boil and cook for 10–15 minutes until they are tender. Drain. Mix the halloumi in a bowl with the oregano and pepper. You do not need to add salt as the cheese is already salty. In a separate bowl whisk the eggs until they are light and full of air. Whisk in the milk.

Put the beans in an even layer in the pastry case, scatter over the cheese mixture ensuring an even spread and a level top. Carefully pour the egg mixture over the beans and cheese. Place in the centre of the oven and cook for 40–45 minutes until the filling is golden brown.

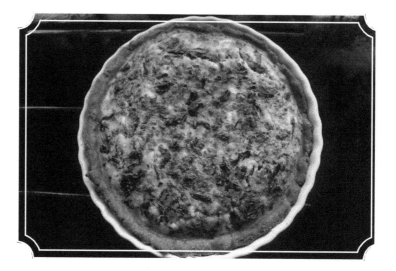

- 1 quantity of shortcrust pastry
- Approx 300 g spinach (cooked weight 140 g)
- 200 g feta cheese
- 1–2 tsp dried oregano
- Ground pepper to taste
- 3–4 eggs, depending on size
- 150 ml full cream milk

This is one of my all-time favourite dishes to make and to eat. I make it with chard and Chinese greens as well, and with an old fashioned English vegetable, Good King Henry – whatever is cropping on the allotment or needs using before it goes to seed. All work well. You can eat it hot straight out of the oven, or at room temperature.

Preheat the oven to 180°C. Press the pastry into a standard 23 cm diameter flan dish, pushing the dough along the bottom and up the sides. You do not need to grease the dish: the pastry will come away cleanly from the sides as it cooks. Another advantage of this wonderful pastry! Trim the top, prick the base all over with a fork, and line with baking parchment and baking beans. Cook for 10 minutes, turn oven down to 160°C and cook for another 10 minutes. Remove beans and return the flan case to the oven for a further 5–10 minutes. Remove from the oven and turn the temperature up to 180°C.

Whilst your pastry is cooking wash the spinach, place in a large saucepan with only the water that clings to its leaves. Wilt it over a low heat. This will only take a couple of minutes but you need to keep turning the leaves to ensure they are all cooked. As soon as the leaves are all limp and still bright green, tip the spinach into a colander and then into a bowl of iced water or run the cold tap over it, ensuring all the spinach is cooled. This is to stop the cooking process. Tip back into the colander and leave to drain. Place the leaves in an old tea towel and wring out the excess water. Do this as thoroughly as you can, or you will end up with a watery flan. Put the ball of spinach you will have ended up with on a kitchen board and cut into 1 cm slices, then turn through 90° and repeat.

In a bowl mash the feta cheese until you have a loose crumbly mixture, add the oregano and pepper and mix well. Add the spinach. You don't need to add salt as the feta is so salty. Mix again. In a separate bowl whisk the eggs until they are light and full of air. Whisk in the milk. Transfer the spinach mixture to the flan and spread evenly over the bottom. Pour the eggs and milk over the spinach and let it settle. Place in the oven and cook for 30–40 minutes until the filling is risen and golden brown. As the flan cools the filling will deflate but this is normal.

This tart can be made 1–2 days ahead of time and refrigerated. Just reheat in a moderate oven for 15–20 minutes. I love to eat it with a crisp salad and new potatoes dressed in olive oil and chopped garlic. And of course a glass of wine.

This is adapted from a recipe in Anna Thomas' *The Vegetarian Epicure*. Anna Thomas is a Polish-American independent filmmaker who wrote this cookery book in the 1970s to help make ends meet. I particularly wanted to keep it in my repertoire because it's great when you have a glut of courgettes. The lemon and thyme I have added make it a very fresh almost spring-like recipe. The original recipe uses sour cream. I prefer to use yoghurt which is lighter but it's up to you. It will keep in the fridge for a couple of days, but is best eaten freshly baked.

- 1 quantity of shortcrust pastry, with added cheese (see note below)
- 100 g pecorino cheese
- 500–600 g courgettes
- 2 eggs, separated
- 200 ml thick Greek style yoghurt
- 1 tsp dried oregano
- 2 sprigs of fresh thyme or ½ tsp of dried thyme

- 50 g walnuts
- 50 g coarse polenta
- Zest of one lemon
- 1 clove of garlic, peeled
- 2 mm thick slice of butter
- Salt
- Pepper

Preheat the oven to 180°C. Grate the pecorino. Mix half the cheese with the pastry **before you add the egg and bring it together**. Press the pastry into a standard 23 cm diameter flan dish, pushing the dough along the bottom and up the sides. You do not need to grease the dish: the pastry will come away cleanly from the sides as it cooks. Trim the top, prick the base all over with a fork, and line with baking parchment and baking beans. Cook for 10 minutes, turn oven down to 160°C and cook for another 10 minutes. Remove beans and cook for a further 5–10 minutes. Remove from the oven and turn the temperature up to 180°C.

Meanwhile, slice the courgettes into discs, approximately 2 mm thick, try to keep them uniform, and place in a large saucepan with one of the sprigs of thyme and a small clove of garlic. If you don't have any fresh thyme just use the garlic. Add boiling salted water and bring to the boil, simmer for 5 minutes then drain and refresh with cold water.

Crush the walnuts either in a food processor, or place in a paper bag and bash with a wooden rolling pin (can be very satisfying). Combine the walnuts and polenta with the remaining 50 g of cheese and lemon zest.

Pick and chop the thyme if you are using fresh thyme. Whip the egg whites until stiff. Mix the yolks with the yoghurt and season. Add the herbs. Fold the whites carefully into this mixture.

Arrange a single layer of courgettes in the bottom of the tart case, pushing them close together. Spread some of the egg and yoghurt mixture over the top. Continue to alternate the layers finishing with the egg mixture. Sprinkle the nut mixture over the top and dot with slivers of butter. Cook in the oven for 40–45 minutes or until the top is golden. It can be eaten hot or cold. It is delicious with a mixed green salad, or with green beans dressed with melted butter and lemon.

In the long hot months of summer 2018, after three days of cooler weather and two lots of long steady rain which broke the weeks' long drought, on another hot day on 1 August we took the bus into town to visit the Wednesday Market at Gloucester Green. We were looking for the woman who sells dhurries. She wasn't there. But wandering among the food stalls we came on one selling Greek produce: a dozen kinds of olives, jars of honey with pieces of honeycomb in them, baklava and feta cheese. He had little cubes of the cheese on taste and proffered them to us as the previous customer repeatedly failed to understand him requesting eleven pounds for his purchases . I love feta cheese and was happy to taste some, but this was something quite different. Soft and creamy, still with a salty tang but not so sharp as the feta you buy in packets. We wanted kalamata olives but also bought some of the cheese. On the way home I decided I would use it in a tart with some of our glut of courgettes, but this time roast them to provide a contrast with the creamy cheese. I did some research when we got home and discovered that this sort of feta is produced in Macedonia and Thrace, but young feta is also creamy and soft. This is the only time I have come across this sort of feta so have no idea how available it is outside the Wednesday Market. You could use curd cheese instead, or something like Boursin would also work.

- *1 quantity of shortcrust pastry*
- *500 g courgettes*
- *3 eggs*
- *200 g of young feta or curd cheese*
- *150 ml full cream milk*
- *1 tsp dried oregano*
- *1 tsp dried mint*
- *Pepper*

Preheat the oven to 180˚C. Press the pastry into a standard 23 cm diameter flan dish, pushing the dough along the bottom and up the sides. You do not need to grease the dish: the pastry will come away cleanly from the sides as it cooks. Trim the top, prick the base all over with a fork, and line with baking parchment and baking beans. Cook for 10 minutes, turn the oven down to 160°C and cook for another 10 minutes. Remove beans and cook for a further 5–10 minutes. Turn the oven up to 180°C.

Slice the courgettes into discs approximately 2 cm thick. Lay them in a single layer on a large baking sheet and pour over roughly one tablespoon of olive oil. Roll the courgette pieces in the oil to make sure they are all coated. Roast in the oven for approximately 20 minutes at 180°C, turn them after 10 minutes. You can cook them at the same time as the pastry case. When they are golden remove from the oven and leave to cool.

Mash the cheese in a clean bowl with the pepper, oregano and mint.

Once the courgettes have cooled enough to handle, chop them into rough 1 cm cubes. Add them to the cheese and gently combine the two.

In a separate bowl whisk the eggs with the milk.

Empty the cheese and courgette mixture into the pastry case and spread it evenly across the base of the tart case. Pour over the egg and milk mixture. Carefully lift the flan dish and cook it in the centre of the oven for 30 minutes, until risen and golden.

This is a nice dish to have at room temperature on a summer's evening with a cooling salad of tomatoes and cucumber.

I used to make a version of this with a puff pastry base topped with sliced tomatoes. As the tomatoes cooked the juices soaked into the pastry and you ended up with an unctuous tart with caramelised tomatoes on the top. In this version you have to cook the tomatoes first but I think it's worth it.

- *1 quantity of shortcrust pastry.*
- *1.5 kg tomatoes*
- *150 g chevre log goats' cheese*
- *50 g parmesan, grated*
- *Large bunch of basil, chopped*
- *Pepper*
- *Salt*
- *Olive oil*

Choose tomatoes that are all about the same size. Lightly oil a large baking tray. Cut the tomatoes in half and lay, cut side up, in the tray. Sprinkle over a little more olive oil and some salt and pepper. Bake in the middle of the oven on 100˚C for 2 hours. Once they have started to blacken on top and have caramelised remove them from the oven. Leave the tomatoes to cool. You can do this the day before you want to make the tart.

To make the tart, preheat the oven to 180°C. Press the pastry into a standard 23 cm diameter flan dish, pushing the dough along the bottom and up the sides. You do not need to grease the dish: the pastry will come away cleanly from the sides as it cooks. Trim the top, prick the base all over with a fork, and line with baking parchment and baking beans. Cook for 10 minutes at 180°C, turn the oven down to 160°C and cook for

another 10 minutes. Remove beans and cook for a further 5–10 minutes. Take out of the oven and leave the pastry case to cool for at least 15 minutes. Turn the oven temperature down to 150°C.

Combine the basil with the parmesan and season with salt and pepper. Spread the mixture on the base of the tart.

Slice the goats' cheese and layer on top of the parmesan.

Now take the tomatoes and starting at the outer edge form a complete circle gently squashing the tomatoes together to cover the cheese layer completely. Make another circle inside the first one in the same way until you have another complete circle. Continue in ever-decreasing circles (the number will depend on the size of your tomatoes) finishing with a single tomato half at the centre.

Repeat, to form a second layer of tomatoes.

Cook for 30 minutes. Again this can be eaten hot or cold. It's lovely with a herby salad. A glass of red wine would also be very nice.

Winter Squash and Chilli Tart

An envelope arrived from the Co-op with my annual divvy plus a booklet outlining some of the community projects it is involved with, and a few recipes, including one for a Sweet Potato and Chilli Tart using, of course, all own brand ingredients. Well, we didn't have any sweet potatoes but boy did we have winter squash. This is an adaptation of the recipe.

- 1 quantity of shortcrust pastry
- 1 small winter squash, approximately 300 g cooked weight
- 2 medium onions
- 2 cloves of garlic
- 1 chilli or 1/8 tsp chilli powder or cayenne pepper
- 1 tsp dried mint
- 3 eggs
- 150 ml full cream milk
- 100 g of cheddar
- 1 tbsp of red wine vinegar
- Pepper

Cut the squash in half and remove the seeds and the stringy fresh around them. Cut into wedges. Peel the wedges and cut into largish chunks. Take a large roasting tray and drizzle the bottom with a couple of tablespoons of olive oil. Arrange the squash in a single layer. Drizzle with a little more oil and sprinkle with salt and pepper.

Preheat the oven to 180°C. Press the pastry into a standard 23 cm diameter flan dish, pressing the dough along the bottom and up the sides. You do not need to grease the dish: the pastry will come away cleaning from the sides and bottom as it cooks. Trim the top, prick the base all over with a fork, and line with baking parchment and baking beans. Put the pastry case in the oven along with the tray of squash. Cook for 10 minutes at 180°C, turn the oven down to 160°C and cook for another 10 minutes. Remove the beans and the squash which should be cooked and starting to caramelise, and cook the pastry case for a further 5–10 minutes. Take out of the oven and leave to cool for at least 15 minutes.

Peel and chop the onions. Peel and finely chop the garlic. Cut the chilli in half if using, de-seed and finely chop. Heat a little olive oil in a small pan, add the onions and a pinch of salt and cook over a low heat until they have softened. Add the garlic, chilli and mint and cook for a further couple of minutes, then add the vinegar and cook until the liquid has all but disappeared. Allow to cool.

Grate the cheese. Whisk the eggs, add the milk and whisk again.

When the squash is cool, dice the chunks into rough 1 cm cubes and place in a bowl. Add the cheese and check the seasoning. Add the onion mix and combine well.

Turn the oven up to 180°C. Put the squash and onion mixture into the pastry case, spreading it evenly across the base. Pour over the egg and milk. Bake for approximately 30 minutes until the tart is golden and set.

Makes 12

These small pies are made in a muffin tin. They are based on pasteles, a Sephardic Jewish speciality. The recipe makes twelve pies.

- *1½ times the quantity of shortcrust pastry.*
  If you are struggling to work this out the quantities are as follows:

- *195 g brown rice flour*
- *45 g tapioca flour*
- *30 g gram flour*
- *1.5 tsp xanthan gum*

- *½ tsp salt*
- *135 g butter or olive oil based spread*
- *2 eggs*

For the filling

- *6 tomatoes approx 4 cm diameter*
- *200 g feta*
- *¼ tsp pepper*
- *1 tsp dried oregano*

Lightly oil a large baking tray. Cut the tomatoes in half and lay, cut side up, in the tray. Sprinkle over a little more olive oil and some salt and pepper. Bake in the middle of the oven at 100°C for 2 hours. Once they have started to blacken on top and have caramelised remove them from the oven. Leave the tomatoes to cool. You can do this the day before you want to make the pies.

Mash the feta with the pepper and oregano.

Sift the flours together in a bowl with the xanthan gum and salt. Rub in the olive oil spread butter until you have the texture of fine breadcrumbs.

Beat the two eggs together in a bowl. Add **three quarters only** to the mix and use a fork to bring it all together in a ball. Reserve the remaining egg for glazing.

Divide the pastry in 12 even pieces. Take the first piece and take off a cherry-sized lump. Roll the larger piece into a rough sphere, press it into the centre of one of the muffin tins and using your fingers ease it out from the centre and up the sides until you have a small pastry case. You don't need to grease the tin: the pastry comes away from the sides as it cooks.

Prick the bottom of each pastry case with a fork. Roll the smaller piece of pastry into a ball in your palms and slightly flatten. Then using your thumb and middle finger, gently flatten the dough from the centre rotating it as you do so until you have a rough circle the size of the top of the muffin tin. This is your pie lid.

Put roughly 2 tsps of the feta mixture in the base of each pastry case. Put a roast half tomato on top. Using a pastry brush or your finger, brush the edge of one side of the pastry lid with egg wash, to provide a seal. Place the lid on top of the pie and push it together with the pastry case. Repeat for all the pies.

Using a sharp knife, cut a small cross in the centre of the pie lid. Use the remaining egg to glaze the top of each pie.

Bake the pies at 180°C in the centre of the oven for 25 minutes. These are very portable so good for school or work lunch boxes and for picnics.

These biscuits use the recipe for short crust pastry. Okay, so they are not perfectly round or an even 1.5 mm all the way through. But rolling out the dough, as we have already established, is not a sensible option. They are easy to make, if a little time consuming, but the recipe lends itself to endless variation depending on your tastes.

- *1 quantity of shortcrust pastry,* **minus the egg**
- *1 egg*
- *20 g sesame seeds*
- *½ tsp coarsely ground black pepper*

Put the sesame seeds in a small heavy frying pan over a low heat. Stirring often, gently roast them.

Once you have rubbed the olive oil spread into the flour mixture add the sesame seeds and pepper and mix thoroughly. Add the egg, mix and bring the dough together.

Turn on your oven to 180°C. Line two largish baking trays with baking parchment.

Take cherry-sized balls of dough, roll them between your palms to get a rough sphere, flatten slightly and then, using your thumbs and middle fingers, starting from the centre, gently flatten the dough, working your way to the outside. The edges will start to crack and split forming what looks like an impressionistic image of a daisy – hence the name.

Lay them out on the baking parchment. You can put them quite close to one another as they don't spread. Bake in the oven for 15–20 minutes until they are golden brown.

Allow them to cool for 5–10 minutes, then transfer to an airtight container. Makes approximately 40 biscuits. You can eat them on their own with a glass of wine or with cheese and chutney and perhaps a glass of cider. I believe that there are now gluten-free beers around but confess I have not tried them. I had already crossed the House.

Tarallini are a Puglian biscuit, often flavoured with fennel. The originals are made with wheat flour and olive oil.

· *1 quantity of shortcrust pastry made with ½ tsp of salt,* **minus the egg**
· *1 egg*
· *1 tsp fennel seeds*
· *1 tsp baking powder*

Add the baking powder to the flours and rub in the olive oil spread. Add the fennel seeds and mix thoroughly. Add the egg, mix and bring the dough together.

Turn on your oven to 180°C. Line two largish baking trays with baking parchment.

Take cherry-sized balls of dough and roll them between your palms to get a rough sphere. Put them on to a flat surface and using the ball of your hand, roll the dough into the shape of a cigarillo. Roll from the middle gently elongating the dough. If the ends taper off too much just push them back into shape. This dough is very malleable and as it contains no gluten does not become over-worked like a wheaten pastry would.

Fold over in a loop as if you were about to tie a knot, and press lightly to secure.

Lay them out on the baking parchment. You can put them quite close to one another: they don't spread.

Bake in the oven for 15–20 minutes until they are golden brown. Allow them to cool for 5–10 minutes. Lovely with a glass of prosecco or a gin and tonic.

They keep in an airtight container for a couple of weeks – if they last that long.

Chapter 2

Flatbread Dough

Bread, hmmm. It's what I miss most. I once tried making bread from a proprietary gluten-free flour following the recipe on the packet. The result came out somewhere between a brioche and a house brick. Gluten free leavened bread recipes call for lots of eggs and milk or so many different flours it gives me a headache thinking about them. None of them are really what I would call bread. However, this flatbread is easy, quick to make and there's no waiting around for the bread to rise. (Keep it under your hat.)

- 75 g gram flour
- 75 g tapioca flour
- ½ tsp salt
- ½ tsp xanthan gum
- 10 ml olive oil or 10 g butter, melted, the choice is yours
- 75 ml water
- Rice flour for rolling out

Sift the flours into a bowl with the xanthan gum (this is important because gram flour clumps and you will end up with lumps if you don't sift). Add salt to the flours and stir.

Make a well in the centre of the flour and pour in the oil or melted butter, stir using a sturdy fork, then add the water, a little at a time and bring it all together. Don't be tempted to put in too much water at a time, particularly towards the end. It takes a bit of work to combine it all. You should end up with a firm but slightly sticky dough.

Cover the bowl with a tea cloth and leave for at least half an hour. Bring together and then divide into six equal pieces. You can use the dough now, but you can also put it in a plastic bag and put it in the fridge: it will keep for several days, and becomes a little easier to handle after a couple of days. It also freezes well. In fact I have taken to making double quantities and freezing them, just taking out a couple at a time so I always have some on hand to use.

This is the dough that I make most often and that I find most useful. You can use it to make pizzette, small savoury pastries such as samosas, wraps for vegetables and salads, and even breadsticks.

The recipe makes six flatbreads, but you can make them one at a time or all together, so if you just want one with your lunch leave the rest of the dough to continue resting and have a freshly cooked one every time. They don't keep well so don't be tempted to cook all six and leave some in the fridge or freezer.

· *1 quantity of flatbread dough.*

Put a large heavy iron frying pan on the largest ring you have on a medium heat. I use a cast iron one.

Turn the dough out onto a work surface which has been sprinkled with rice flour. Divide into 6. Take the first piece of dough and roll it into a rough ball. Put it on the work surface and press it flat. Keep turning the dough over to make sure that it is covered on both sides with flour.

Once you have a circle of about 10 cm sprinkle the top with flour and, with a rolling pin, gently roll it out to make a rough 15 cm circle. Keep making sure that you have sufficient flour on both sides of the dough.

Pick up the flatbread and pat it between your hands to remove as much flour as possible. Put the flatbread into the frying pan to cook. You do not need to use any oil. Meanwhile start making the second flatbread.

The flatbread in the pan will start to bubble in places. After 2–3 minutes flip it over to cook on the other side. Each side should be golden brown in spots and slightly puffed up in places.

Remove and cover with a tea cloth to keep warm whilst you continue with the other flatbreads. If you get a build-up of flour in the pan, scrape out as much as you can and continue with the cooking. Eat immediately.

These flatbreads are fantastically versatile. I use them as a pitta bread substitute to eat with salads, sauces and kofte.

- 75 g gram flour
- 75 g tapioca flour
- ½ tsp salt
- ½ tsp xanthan gum
- 10 ml olive oil or 10 g butter, melted, the choice is yours
- 75 ml water
- ½ tsp fennel seeds
- ½ tsp cumin seeds
- 3–4 curry leaves crumbled
- Rice flour for rolling

Put fennel and cumin seeds in a small pan over a low heat and toast for a couple of minutes. Tip them into mortar and grind with a pestle to break them up: you are not trying to grind them to a powder.

Sift the flours and the xanthan gum into a bowl, add the cumin and fennel seeds, and crumbled curry leaves to the flours and stir.

Add the olive oil or melted butter, stir, and then the water, a little at a time and bring it all together. You should end up with a firm but slightly sticky dough. Cover the bowl with a tea cloth and leave for at least half an hour.

Put a large cast iron frying pan on a high heat.

Turn the dough out onto a work surface which has been sprinkled with rice flour. Divide into 6. Take the first piece of dough and roll it into a rough ball. Put it on the work surface and press it flat. Keep turning the dough over to make sure that it is covered on both sides with flour, otherwise it will stick.

Once you have a circle of about 10 cm sprinkle the top with flour and with, a rolling pin, gently roll it out to make a rough 15 cm circle.

Pick up the flatbread and pat it between your hands to remove as much flour as possible. Put the flatbread into the frying pan to cook. You do not need to use any oil. Meanwhile start making the second flatbread.

The flatbread in the pan will start to bubble in places. After about 2 minutes, flip it over to cook on the other side. Each side should be golden brown in spots and slightly puffed up in places.

Remove and cover with a tea cloth to keep warm whilst you continue with the other flatbreads. If you get a build-up of flour in the pan, scrape out as much as you can and continue with the cooking. Eat immediately.

～～ Spiced Yoghurt Scrambled Eggs on Flatbreads ～～

You can make this with or without the spices. In that case substitute a pinch of ground black pepper for the spices. Equally you can serve it on a plain flatbread. Either way it is delicious.

For each person you will need:

- *1 egg*
- *2 tbsps yoghurt*
- *1/8 tsp of salt*
- *1/8 tsp of ground cumin*

- *1/8 tsp of ground cinnamon*
- *1/8 tsp of paprika*
- *A knob of butter*
- *1 Indian flatbread.*

Crack the egg in a small bowl, add the yoghurt, salt and spices and roughly mix together.

Heat a heavy frying pan. Roll out your flatbread and put it in the hot pan *(see on page 42)*.

In a non-stick pan heat the butter. When it has melted add the egg mixture and turn from time to time until it is cooked through.

Meanwhile turn your flatbread when it starts to puff up.

Serve the egg on the flatbread.

～～ Pizzetta ～～

The idea for this came from the Russell Norman's cookbook *Polpo*. At the Polpo restaurants they make pizzetta, a smaller version of pizza. This version is very quick to make and you don't need a pizza stone to cook them: I've tried them on a stone and on baking sheets and you get a better bake with the baking sheets.

Pizza Bianca, properly, is a Roman street food, a simple pizza dough dressed with salt and olive oil. This is a bit more elaborate and is inspired by Norman Russell's Pizzetta Bianca in *Polpo*. He uses 'cheap' mozzarella which he says works better than high quality buffalo mozzarella in this recipe, and adds onions. I use halloumi because I always have some in the fridge, along with my flatbread dough, so it's easy to knock up when I fancy it. I also add chilli, just because I can. Leave it out if you don't like it. From thinking about it to eating it takes roughly 30 minutes. How good is that?

Line two large baking sheets with baking parchment. Turn the oven to its highest setting (mine is 230°C). If your baking sheets are not big enough to accommodate three pizzette each, you may need to do these in batches.

- · *1 quantity of basic flatbread dough*
- · *200 g grated halloumi cheese*
- · *6 small shallots, finely sliced*

Finely sliced fresh chilli (optional)

This recipe makes six pizzette but you could make fewer and put the rest of the dough in a plastic bag in the fridge. I can fit three on a large baking sheet.

Turn the dough out onto a work surface which has been sprinkled with rice flour. Roll the dough out as you would for flatbread and pat off as much of the rice flour as you can. Put the bases on the baking sheets. Sprinkle some cheese over each base, sparingly: if you put too much on it won't cook well. Evenly spread the shallot and chilli over the cheese. Cook for about 5 minutes.

Potato pizza is a thing in Italy. Once again inspired by *Polpo* here is a recipe for one.

Line two large baking sheets with baking parchment. Turn the oven to its highest setting (mine is 230°C). If your baking sheets are not big enough to accommodate three pizzette each, you may need to do these in batches.

· *1 quantity of basic flatbread dough*
· *200 g grated halloumi cheese*
· *36 green olives*
· *6 small potatoes or 3 medium ones*
· *Chilli flakes (optional)*

This recipe makes six pizzette but you could make fewer and put the rest of the dough in a plastic bag in the fridge. I can fit three on a large baking sheet.

Boil the potatoes and, once cool, slice into 2 mm thick slices. Or use leftovers. Slice the olives in half and cut the halves into three.

Turn the dough out onto a work surface which has been sprinkled with rice flour. Roll the dough out as you would for flatbread and pat off as much of the rice flour as you can. Put the bases on the baking sheets.

Sprinkle some cheese over each base, sparingly: if you put too much on it won't cook well. Evenly spread the potato and olive pieces over the cheese. Sprinkle over the chilli flakes if you are using them. Cook for about 5 minutes.

Pear and Blue Cheese Pizetta

Buying some blue cheese at the Oxford Cheese Company stall in the Covered Market, I said it was for cooking. Cooking what? I was making pear and blue cheese parcels. The woman serving me told me that she made pear and blue cheese pizza. Really? I must try that.

- *1 quantity flatbread dough*
- *1 onion*
- *20 g walnuts*
- *75 g of sliced pear*
- *75 g gorgonzola*

This recipe makes six pizzette but you could make fewer and put the rest of the dough in a plastic bag in the fridge. I can fit three on a large baking sheet.

Line two large baking sheets with baking parchment. Turn the oven to its highest setting (mine is 230°C). If your baking sheets are not big enough to accommodate three pizzette each, you may need to do these in batches.

Slice the onion finely. Put a glug of olive oil in a small pan on a low heat. Add the onions and a pinch of salt. Cook the onions slowly until they are soft and starting to caramelise.

Chop the walnuts. Cut the pear slices into small pieces.

Turn the dough out onto a work surface which has been sprinkled with rice flour. Roll the dough out as you would for flatbread and pat off as much of the rice flour as you can. Put the bases on the baking sheets.

Divide the onions evenly between the flatbreads. Sprinkle on the nuts and pears. Crumble the blue cheese over the top.

Cook in the oven for about 5 minutes keeping a careful watch to make sure they don't burn.

Mushroom Wraps (Vg)

- *1 quantity of flatbread dough*
- *300 g button mushrooms*
- *3 cloves garlic*
- *½ tsp salt*
- *1 tbsp lemon juice*
- *Olive oil*

Finely slice the mushrooms and finely chop the garlic. In a frying pan or small casserole heat a good glug of olive oil and add the mushrooms. Once the mushrooms have cooked add the garlic and cook for 2 more minutes. Add the lemon juice and salt. Continue to cook on a fairly high heat to evaporate the liquid.

Meanwhile cook the flatbreads in a heavy bottomed frying pan (see the Basic Flatbread recipe). Divide the mushroom mixture between the flatbreads, fold over and eat. It's quite a messy operation but tastes delicious.

This is a quick dish to make for a light lunch. If you don't like the spices you can omit them and replace with a little freshly ground pepper.

- *1 plain or Indian flatbread*
- *1 small to medium onion*
- *Pinch of cumin seeds*
- *Pinch of mustard seeds*
- *A few fenugreek seeds*
- *Pinch of salt*
- *Olive oil*

Peel and slice the onion. In a small saucepan heat a little olive oil and add the spices. When they start to colour and sizzle add the sliced onion and a pinch of salt. Cook on a very low heat for 15–20 minutes until the onion softens and begins to caramelise.

Cook the flatbread in a heavy bottomed frying pan (see the Basic Flatbread recipe). Pile the onions onto the flatbread, fold over and consume.

Follow it with a fresh salad or some fruit.

Spinach Samosas (Vg)

I used to make samosas using shortcrust pastry and would bake them in the oven rather than fry them. After making pizzette I realised quite how malleable this dough is and thought I would try making small savoury pastries using it. And it works – hurrah! The turmeric in the filling turns the pastry a lovely golden colour. The filling is adapted from Madhur Jaffrey's Sookhe aloo in *An Invitation to Indian Cooking*.

Makes 12

- *1 quantity of basic flatbread dough*

For the filling:

- *150 g spinach (cooked weight)*
- *1 small onion*
- *½ tsp cumin seeds*
- *½ tsp mustard seeds*
- *½ tsp fennel seeds*
- *10 fenugreek seeds*
- *1/8 tsp asafoetida*
- *¼ tsp turmeric*
- *1/8 tsp cayenne pepper*
- *½ tsp salt*
- *4 tbsp sunflower oil*
- *Juice of half a lemon*
- *Rice flour for rolling out the dough*

To make the filling:

Wash the spinach in plenty of cold water and remove any tough stems.

Drain and put the spinach in a large saucepan with only the water that clings to its leaves. Wilt it over a low heat. This will only take a couple of minutes but you need to keep turning the leaves to ensure they are all cooked.

As soon as the leaves are all limp and still bright green, tip the spinach into a colander and then into a bowl of iced water or run under the cold tap. This is to stop the cooking process. Tip back into the colander and leave to drain.

Place the leaves in an old tea towel and wring out the excess water. Do this as thoroughly as you can, or you will end up with a watery filling.

Put the ball of spinach you will have ended up with on a kitchen board and cut into 1 cm slices, then turn through 90° and repeat. Chop the onion.

In a large frying pan or casserole dish heat the oil. Add the asafoetida and as it starts to fizz add the cumin, mustard, fennel and fenugreek seeds. Once they start to pop add the onion and turn the heat to low and add a little salt. Once the onion has softened, add the turmeric, and cayenne pepper. Stir every few minutes to make sure it cooks evenly and does not stick. Turn off the heat and pour over the lemon juice. Mix well and add a little more salt if needed.

To assemble the samosas:

Line two baking sheets with parchment.

Turn the dough out onto a work surface which has been sprinkled with rice flour. Divide into 6 and return the pieces to the plastic bag.

Flour a board or work surface with the rice flour. Take the first piece of dough and roll it into a rough ball. Put it on the work surface and press it flat. Keep turning the dough over and making sure that it is covered on both sides with flour. Once you have a circle of about 10 cm sprinkle the top with flour and, with a rolling pin, gently roll it out to make a rough 15 cm circle.

Fill a small glass or cup with water. Take the circle of dough and cut it in half so that you have two semicircles. *(The process is illustrated on page 53)* Now take one of the semicircles and place it with the straight side facing towards you. At the midpoint of this line fold first one half to the middle, so that the end of flat side meets the middle of the semicircle.

Dip your finger in the water and moisten the edge of the folded side which is now perpendicular to you. Fold the other half in the same way, overlapping the first half. You now have a rough triangle. Put it in the palm of your hand and with your other hand open it into a cone. Using your thumb and first finger carefully press the fold together down to the base of the cone.

Fill the cone with 1–2 teaspoons of the filling. Once again holding the samosa in your palm so the whole thing flattens slightly, moisten the inside of the top back edge with water and fold it over the front edge and roughly crimp. Place on one of the baking sheets. Repeat with the other half of the circle. Take another ball of dough from the bag and repeat the process, always keeping the other pieces inside the plastic bag to stop them drying out.

Bake in a preheated oven at 180°C for approximately 20 minutes or until golden.

Potato and Pea Samosas (Vg)

The filling is from a Madhur Jaffrey samosa recipe in her book *Eastern Vegetarian Cooking*. If you cannot source amchoor use the juice of half a lemon instead.

- 1 quantity of flatbread dough
- 120 g boiled potatoes
- 120 g cooked peas
- 1 small onion
- A piece of fresh ginger roughly 1.5 cm cubed
- ½ a large bunch of fresh coriander
- 2 cloves garlic
- 1 fresh chilli
- ¼ tsp of cayenne pepper
- ½–1 tsp salt
- 1 tsp ground coriander
- 2 tsps ground cumin
- 1 tbsp amchoor (dried, ground mango)
- ½ tsp anardana (dried pomegranate seeds)
- 2 tbsp of sunflower oil

Cut the potatoes into 1 cm rough cubes. Chop the onion.

Heat the oil in a heavy based pan on a low heat. Add the onion with a pinch of salt and cook until soft. Add garlic, ginger and chilli and cook for another two minutes. Add the dry spices and cook for a further two minutes. Add the peas and potatoes and combine everything. Test the level of salt and adjust as necessary. Mix well and leave to cool.

To assemble the samosas:

Line two baking sheets with parchment.

Turn the dough out onto a work surface which has been sprinkled with rice flour. Divide into 6 and return the pieces to the plastic bag.

Take the first piece of dough and roll it into a rough ball. Put it on the work surface and press it flat. Keep turning the dough over and making sure that it is covered on both sides with flour. Once you have a circle of about 10 cm sprinkle the top with flour and, with a rolling pin, gently roll it out to make a rough 15 cm circle.

Fill a small glass or cup with water. Take the circle of dough and cut it in half so that you have two semicircles. *(The process is illustrated on page 53)* Now take one of the semicircles and place it with the straight side facing towards you. At the midpoint of this line fold first one half to the middle, so that the end of flat side meets the middle of the semicircle.

Dip your finger in the water and moisten the edge of the folded side which is now perpendicular to you. Fold the other half in the same way, overlapping the first half. You now have a rough triangle. Put it in the palm of your hand and with your other hand open it into a cone. Using your thumb and first finger carefully press the fold together down to the base of the cone.

Fill the cone with 1–2 teaspoons of the filling. Once again holding the samosa in your palm so the whole thing flattens slightly, moisten the inside of the top back edge with water and fold it over the front edge and roughly crimp. Place on one of the baking sheets. Repeat with the other half of the circle. Take another ball of dough from the bag and repeat the process, always keeping the other pieces inside the plastic bag to stop them drying out.

Bake in a preheated oven at 180°C for approximately 20 minutes or until golden.

The filling is adapted from a Madhur Jaffrey recipe for Potatoes with Whole Spices and Sesame Seeds in her book *Eastern Vegetarian Cooking*. If you cannot source amchoor use the juice of half a lemon instead. Use just one chilli, de-seeded for a subtle heat, or both with or without the seeds depending on how hot you like your food.

Makes 12

- 1 quantity of flatbread dough
- 1 small to medium Winter Squash
- 1 tsp cumin seeds
- 10 fenugreek seeds
- 1 tsp black mustard seeds
- Vegetable oil
- A pinch of ground asafoetida
- 1 or 2 chillies
- 1 tbsp Sesame seeds
- A pinch of ground turmeric
- Appox ½ tsp salt
- A pinch of ground black pepper
- 1 tsp amchoor

Preheat your oven to 230°C. Cut the squash in half and remove the seeds and the stringy fresh around them. Cut into wedges. Peel the wedges and cut into largish chunks. Take a large roasting tray and drizzle the bottom with a couple of tablespoons of olive oil. Arrange the squash in a single layer. Drizzle with a little more oil and sprinkle with salt and pepper. Roast for approximately 30 minutes until the squash is starting to darken at the edges. Remove from the oven and allow to cool.

Heat the oil in a small saucepan or frying pan. When it's hot, add the asafoetida, allow it to sizzle for a couple of seconds then add the cumin, fenugreek and mustard seeds. Stir. Add the chilli and stir well, and cook for a couple of minutes before adding the sesame seeds. Now add the turmeric, continuing to stir. Add the amchoor and keep stirring until the sesame seeds begin to change colour. Add salt and pepper to taste. Remove from the heat.

Cut the cooled squash into approximately 1 cm cubes put into a large bowl. Add the spices and combine well.

To assemble the samosas:

Line two baking sheets with parchment.

Turn the dough out onto a work surface which has been sprinkled with rice flour. Divide into 6 and return the pieces to the plastic bag.

Take the first piece of dough and roll it into a rough ball. Put it on the work surface and press it flat. Keep turning the dough over and making sure that it is covered on both sides with flour. Once you have a circle of about 10 cm sprinkle the top with flour and, with a rolling pin, gently roll it out to make a rough 15 cm circle.

Fill a small glass or cup with water. Take the circle of dough and cut it in half so that you have two semicircles. *(The process is illustrated on page 53)* Now take one of the semicircles and place it with the straight side facing towards you. At the midpoint of this line fold first one half to the middle, so that the end of flat side meets the middle of the semicircle.

Dip your finger in the water and moisten the edge of the folded side which is now perpendicular to you. Fold the other half in the same way, overlapping the first half. You now have a rough triangle. Put it in the palm of your hand, and with your other hand open it into a cone. Using your thumb and first finger carefully press the fold together down to the base of the cone.

Fill the cone with 1–2 teaspoons of the filling. Once again holding the samosa in your palm so the whole thing flattens slightly, moisten the inside of the top back edge with water and fold it over the front edge and roughly crimp. Place on one of the baking sheets. Repeat with the other half of the circle. Take another ball of dough from the bag and repeat the process, always keeping the other pieces inside the plastic bag to stop them drying out.

Bake in a preheated oven at 180°C for approximately 20 minutes or until golden.

Börek are Turkish pastries made sometimes with pie dough, sometimes with flaky pastry and sometimes with bread dough. You can use spinach instead of chard if you prefer.

Makes 24

- A double quantity of flatbread dough
- 200 g chard leaves
- 200 g feta cheese
- Zest of 1 lemon
- 10 allspice berries, ground
- 1 tsp oregano
- ¼ tsp black pepper
- Brown rice flour for rolling the dough

Wash the chard and drain, removing thick stems. You can keep these and cook them separately. Drain and put the chard in a large saucepan with only the water that clings to its leaves. Wilt it over a low heat. This will only take a couple of minutes but you need to keep turning the leaves to ensure they are all cooked.

As soon as the leaves are all limp and still bright green, tip the chard into a colander and then into a bowl of iced water or run under the cold tap. This is to stop the cooking process. Tip back into the colander and leave to drain.

Place the leaves in an old tea towel and wring out the excess water. Do this as thoroughly as you can, or you will end up with a watery filling.

Put the feta cheese in a bowl and mash well with a fork. Grate the lemon zest into the bowl, add the allspice, oregano and black pepper.

Put the ball of chard you now have on a chopping board and with a sharp knife cut it into slices then turn the ball through 90° and slice again. Add to the bowl and mix all the ingredients well until combined.

Line two largish baking sheets with baking parchment. Turn the dough out onto a work surface which has been sprinkled with rice flour and divide in two. Take one half and divide into 6 as though you were making flatbreads. Repeat with the other half. Roll each piece lightly in flour and put them in a plastic bag so that they don't dry out. Take the first piece of dough and divide it into 2 pieces. Roll each piece into a ball. Place the first ball on the work surface and sprinkle well with rice flour, flatten slightly then roll out with a rolling pin as you would for a flatbread, into a rough circle no more than 10 cm across. Make sure it is not too thin: it should be about 1.5 mm thick.

Fill a small glass or cup with water. Take the circle of dough and with your finger wet the edge all the way round. Using a teaspoon place about two teaspoonfuls of the mixture in the middle of the dough, spreading it slightly to each side. Fold the dough over so you have a pasty shape and press the edges together. Place on one of the baking sheets. Repeat with all the other pieces.

When you are nearing the end of preparing the pastries set the oven on to 180°C. Cook them for approximately 15 minutes until the pastries start to colour.

Pear and Gorgonzola Parcels

The idea for these came from a recipe in a French magazine using puff pastry. Obviously that is not an option, and I can see why they used it because the hot bubbling cheese would soak into that pastry. However, flatbread dough makes an acceptable alternative. Some of the cheese will ooze out onto the baking parchment as they cook. Just wait until it cools a bit before scraping it off with your fingers: cook's perk. Delicious.

Makes about 24

- *A double quantity of flatbread dough.*
- *200 g gorgonzola*
- *170 g poached pears*
- *Black pepper*

You could use a different blue cheese if you prefer. I asked my lovely cheesemonger which she suggested for making this dish and she suggested gorgonzola so that's what I used. Now you don't have to make the parcels this shape, I just rather liked it. You could easily make them like little pasties, like the börek.

Remove any hard rind from the cheese and then put it into a small bowl and roughly break up with a fork. Dice the pears into rough 1 cm cubes and place in a separate bowl. Add a couple of pinches of black pepper and mix so the peppers are evenly coated with the pepper. Add to the cheese and mix again. It won't combine smoothly. You're really just redistributing the pears amongst the cheese.

Line two largish baking sheets with baking parchment. Sprinkle a chopping board or kitchen surface with brown rice flour, place the flatbread dough on it and divide in two. Take one half and divide into 6 as though you were making flatbreads. Repeat with the other half. Roll each piece lightly in flour and put them in a plastic bag so that they don't dry out. Take the first piece of dough and divide it into 2 pieces. Roll each piece into a ball. Place the first ball on the work surface and sprinkle well with rice flour, flatten slightly and then roll out with a rolling pin as you would for a flatbread, into a rough circle no more than 10 cm across. Make sure it is not too thin: it should be about 1.5 mm thick. It's best not to roll out all the dough, I usually make 4 rounds at a time.

Fill a small glass or cup with water. Take the circle of dough and with your finger wet the edge all the way round. Using a teaspoon place about 1½ tsps of the mixture in the middle of the dough, spreading it slightly to each side. Bring the parcel together as though you were making a pasty, but only pinch ¼ of the length on each side. Then fold each side together so that you have a four cornered parcel. Place on one of the baking sheets. Repeat with all the other pieces.

Once you are on your last few pastries, preheat the oven to 180˚C. When it is up to temperature place the baking sheets in the oven, and bake for approximately 10–15 minutes, checking regularly. They should be golden and yes, there will be cheese on the baking parchment.

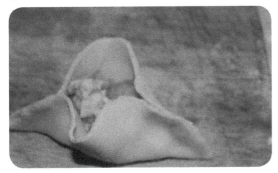
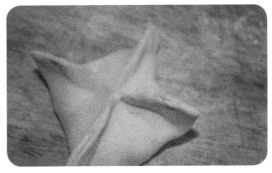

Bread sticks are a very pleasant pre-dinner nibble, especially if you are having a glass of prosecco.

Makes 24

· *1 quantity of flatbread dough.*

Line 2 large baking sheets with baking parchment. Preheat the oven to 230°C.

Put the dough on a lightly floured board and divide it into 6 roughly equal parts as you would for making flatbreads. Roll each section into a fat sausage and divide that into 4 equal pieces.

Using your hands roll each piece into a stick about 12 cm long and ½ cm diameter. Lay the sticks out on the baking sheets and put into the oven.

They take about 5 minutes but keep an eye on them to make sure they don't burn. They don't keep well so I suggest you only make as many as you need and gobble them all up. Lovely with hummus and of course that glass of prosecco.

Chapter 3

~~~~~~~~~~~~~~~~~~~~~~~~~~

Pancakes , Crackers
and Muffins

This batter will keep in the fridge for a number of days, so you can make a few for a snack and enjoy the rest over the next day or two. They are good with hummus or cream cheese, and they should be eaten freshly made.

Makes 12–16

- 100 g gram flour
- 110 ml water
- 1 tsp brown sugar
- Pinch of salt
- ½ tsp bicarbonate of soda
- ½ tsp white wine vinegar
- Olive oil for frying

Sift the flour into a bowl with the bicarbonate of soda (this is important because gram flour clumps and you will end up with lumps if you don't sift it). Stir in the salt, sugar and vinegar. Add the water gradually. 100 ml gives you the consistency of beaten double cream. You need to go just past that so the batter pours but is still quite thick.

Leave it to stand for at least 10 minutes to let the vinegar react with the bicarbonate of soda. When you see bubbles rising the batter is ready.

In a large cast iron or non-stick frying pan heat a teaspoon of olive oil. Make sure the bottom of the pan is covered.

Take a tablespoon of the mixture and pour into the pan to make a small scotch pancake-sized blini. Repeat several times but do not overcrowd the pan as you need room to flip them over. I usually cook 4 at a time.

When they are golden brown on the underside flip them carefully over to cook on the other side. If they are sticking to the pan when you try to turn them they are not yet ready. They should come away from the pan easily. When they are done put them on a warmed plate whilst you cook the others.

If you are using a cast iron pan, turn the heat down before doing the next batch, as the pan retains heat really well and will become too hot. Re-oil the pan between batches.

Make as many as you want to eat and keep the remaining batter in the fridge. It will keep for up to a week this way. Just take it out half an hour before you want to use it and give it a good stir.

These are quick to make for breakfast and delicious with marmalade.

Makes 12–16

- 100 g gram flour
- 115–120 ml water
- 1 tbsp brown sugar
- Pinch of salt
- ½ tsp bicarbonate of soda
- ½ tsp white wine vinegar
- 1 tsp ground cinnamon
- Olive oil for frying

Sift the flour into a bowl with the bicarbonate of soda and cinnamon (this is important because gram flour clumps and you will end up with lumps if you don't sift). Stir in the salt, sugar and vinegar. Add the water gradually. About 100 ml gives you the consistency of beaten double cream. You need to go just past that so the batter pours but is still quite thick.

Leave it to stand for at least 10 minutes to let the vinegar react with the bicarbonate of soda. When you see bubbles rising the batter is ready.

In a large cast iron or non-stick frying pan heat a teaspoon of olive oil. Make sure the bottom of the pan is covered.

Take a tablespoon of the mixture and pour into the pan to make a small scotch pancake sized blini. Repeat several times but do not overcrowd the pan as you need room to flip them over. I usually cook 4 at a time.

When they are golden brown on the underside flip them carefully over to cook on the other side. If they are sticking to the pan when you try to turn them they are not yet ready. They should come away from the pan easily. When they are done put them on a warmed plate whilst you cook the others.

If you are using a cast iron pan, turn the heat down before doing the next batch, as the pan retains heat really well and will become too hot. Re-oil the pan between batches.

Make as many as you want to eat and keep the remaining batter in the fridge. It will keep for up to a week this way. Just take it out half an hour before you want to use it and give it a good stir.

~~~~~~~~~~~~~~~~ *Crepes (Vg)* ~~~~~~~~~~~~~~~~

This is based on a recipe from Madhur Jaffrey's *Eastern Vegetarian Cooking*. It is similar to the *socca* of Nice. You need to use a heavy or a non-stick frying pan which has a lid.

Makes 4

- 100 g gram flour
- ½ tsp salt
- ½ tsp turmeric
- ½ tsp cumin

- 300 ml water
- Approximately 4 tsps of sunflower oil for cooking

Sift the gram flour with the spices into a large bowl (this is important because gram flour clumps and you will end up with lumps if you don't sift) and add the salt. Add the water gradually.

Heat a tsp of oil in a 20 cm heavy or non-stick frying pan on a low heat until hot. Pour approximately 100 ml of the batter into the pan and swirl to cover the bottom of the pan. Cover the pan with a saucepan lid and cook the pancake for approximately 8 minutes. Carefully ease up the edges of the crepe with an egg-slice and transfer it to a warmed plate. Cover to keep warm whilst you make the other crepes. You will need to add a teaspoon of oil to the pan for each crepe.

These are lovely spread with chilli jelly and filled with chopped tomatoes and cucumber in the summer, or wrapped around sliced mushrooms cooked just with a little salt and lemon juice in the autumn. Omit the turmeric and cayenne and serve with lemon juice and a sprinkling of sugar on Shrove Tuesday.

I like to have these for breakfast occasionally, with marmalade or crab-apple jelly. Like the batter for the blinis this will keep in the fridge for a number of days, so you can make a few for breakfast and enjoy the rest over the next morning or two. They should be eaten freshly made.

- *50 g gram flour*
- *50 g tapioca flour*
- *50 ml water*
- *2 tbsp sugar*
- *½ tsp bicarbonate of soda*

- *½ tsp cinnamon*
- *½ tsp white wine vinegar*
- *Pinch of salt*
- *1 egg, beaten*

Sift the flours into a bowl with the bicarbonate of soda (this is important because gram flour clumps and you will end up with lumps if you don't sift). Stir in the salt, sugar, cinnamon and vinegar.

Add the beaten egg and beat into the flours. Add the water gradually until you have a paste of a pouring consistency. Leave it to stand for at least 10 minutes to let the vinegar react with the bicarbonate of soda. When you see bubbles rising the batter is ready.

In a large cast iron frying pan heat a teaspoon of olive oil. Wait until the pan is really hot (test with a teaspoon of the mixture).

Take a tablespoon of the mixture and pour into the pan to make a small pancake. Repeat several times but do not overcrowd the pan as you need room to flip them over. I usually cook 4 at a time. Small bubbles will appear on the surface of the pancake as it cooks. Once these appear evenly over the surface they will be ready to flip over. When both sides are golden brown they are done. Put them on a warmed plate whilst you cook the others.

If you are using a cast iron pan, turn the heat down before doing the next batch, as the pan retains heat really well and will become too hot. Re-oil the pan between batches.

Using tapioca flour improves the moisture holding quality of the mixture so these pancakes will keep better and can be reheated. Store them in the fridge overnight and refresh under the grill. They can also be frozen and reheated from frozen.

Breakfast Cereal (Vg)

Now you can of course eat Cornflakes or Rice Krispies but those cereals are packed with sugar. If you can eat oats muesli is a good option. If, like me, you cannot eat oats this is an alternative.

- Puffed Rice
- Peanuts
- Raw cashews
- Pumpkin seeds
- Raisins

You can get puffed rice in Middle Eastern and Asian shops. Health food shops such as Holland & Barrett also stock them.

Empty the puffed rice into a shallow baking tray and bake in a moderate oven for 5–10 minutes. I do this whilst I am using the oven the cook something else.

Put a handful of the peanuts, cashews and pumpkin seeds in a separate shallow baking tray and do the same. Leave to cool.

When the rice and nuts are cool store them in separate airtight containers. I use an old glass jar for the nut mix.

I have deliberately not given you amounts. The rice comes in different size bags so just get whatever you can. People have different tastes as to how much rice to nuts and fruit they like. Experiment until you find what suits you.

To assemble, take a cereal dispenser and fill it two-thirds full of puffed rice. Add the roasted nuts and seeds and some raisins. Gently tip the container back and forth to mix.

You can of course use any mixture of seeds, nuts and fruit. I have used walnuts, hazelnuts, sunflower seeds and cranberries as substitutes or you might like to use chopped dried apricots and figs. Use as many or as few as you wish. And in the summer it is lovely topped with fresh berries.

Serve with cold milk.

Rice cakes are very nice, but in truth, not very filling. These are quite substantial and are very good with cheese, hummus and with peanut butter. It's up to you how large you make them. You can use any combination of nuts and seeds you want, but you do need to use 100 g of flour or the mixture will not hold together and the end result will be very crumbly. Try using different spices or just make them plain. Here are three combinations I use to get you started.

Pumpkin Seed Crackers

Makes around 30–40 (depending on how large you make them)

- 100 g brown rice flour
- 100 g pumpkin seeds
- 100 g peanuts
- 1 egg
- 2 tbsp water
- 1 tsp sea salt
- 1 tsp ajwain seeds (optional)

Ajwain seeds are an Indian spice available in all good Eastern grocery shops. If you cannot get hold of them substitute black pepper or omit altogether.

Place the pumpkin seeds and peanuts into a blender and blend until they are the consistency of fine cous cous.

Tip into a bowl, add the flour, ajwain seeds and sea salt and mix thoroughly. Add the egg and water and, using a large fork, combine everything into a stiff paste. If it seems a little crumbly add a bit more water.

Preheat the oven to 180. Line 2 flat baking trays with baking parchment. It is important that they don't have raised sides because you are going to roll the biscuits out on the baking sheet. If you don't have a flat baking sheet do it on a cool work top and transfer the sheets to your baking trays *carefully* after you have rolled it out but before you cut the dough.

Divide the dough into 2 rough balls and place them directly on the parchment papers. Cover with another piece of baking parchment and roll them out to a thickness of about 1.5–2 mm. Carefully remove the top sheet of parchment.

Use a sharp kitchen knife to cut through the pastry making rough rectangles. They will be uneven, but there is no way round this and anyway it's part of their charm.

Bake for 15 minutes. Remove from the oven and, using a palette knife, gently ease the crackers apart. Those on the outside will be more browned so remove these to a cooling rack and return the rest to the oven and cook for a further 5–10 minutes until they are golden brown.

Once cool store in an airtight container. They keep for several weeks, provided the container is airtight.

Makes around 30–40 (depending on how large you make them)

- 100 g walnuts
- 100 g fine polenta
- 50 g sesame seeds
- 50 g gram flour

- 1 egg
- 1–2 tbsp water
- 1 tsp sea salt
- ½ tsp black pepper

Place the walnuts and sesame seeds into a blender and blend until they are the consistency of fine cous cous.

Sift in the gram flour into a bowl, add the polenta, pulverized walnut and sesame seeds, sea salt and black pepper and mix thoroughly. Add the egg and water and, using a large fork, combine everything into a stiff paste. If it seems a little crumbly add a bit more water.

Preheat the oven to 180°C.

Line 2 flat baking trays with baking parchment. It is important that they are flat because you are going to roll the biscuits out on the baking sheet. If you don't have a flat baking sheet do it on a cool work top and transfer the sheets to your baking trays *carefully* after you have rolled it out but before you cut the dough.

Divide the dough into 2 rough balls and place them directly on the parchment papers. Cover with another piece of baking parchment and roll them out to a thickness of about 1.5–2 mm. Carefully remove the top sheet of parchment.

Use a sharp kitchen knife to cut through the pastry making rough rectangles. They will be uneven, but there is no way round this and anyway it's part of their charm.

Bake for 15 minutes. After 15 minutes remove from the oven and, using a palette knife, gently ease the crackers apart. Those on the outside will be more browned so remove these to a cooling rack and return the rest to the oven and cook for a further 5–10 minutes until they are golden brown.

Once cool store in an airtight container. They keep for several weeks, provided the container is airtight.

Makes around 30–40 (depending on how large you make them)

- 100 g hazelnuts
- 100 g sunflower seeds
- 100 g gram flour
- 1 egg
- 1 tbsp water
- 1 tsp sea salt
- 1 tsp nigella seeds

Nigella seeds are sold in Asian grocery shops as Kalonji. If you cannot get hold of them substitute ½ tsp of ground black pepper or omit altogether.

Place the hazelnuts and sunflower seeds into a blender and blend until they are the consistency of fine cous cous,

Sift in the gram flour into a bowl, add the pulverised hazelnuts and sunflower seeds, sea salt and nigella seeds and mix thoroughly. Add the egg and water and, using a large fork, combine everything into a stiff paste. If it seems a little crumbly add a bit more water.

Preheat the oven to 180˚C.

Line 2 flat baking trays with baking parchment. It is important that they are flat because you are going to roll the biscuits out on the baking sheet. If you don't have a flat baking sheet do it on a cool work top and transfer the sheets to your baking trays *carefully* after you have rolled it out but before you cut the dough.

Divide the dough into 2 rough balls and place them directly on the parchment papers. Cover with another piece of baking parchment and roll them out to a thickness of about 1.5–2 mm. Carefully remove the top sheet of parchment.

Use a sharp kitchen knife to cut through the pastry making rough rectangles. They will be uneven, but there is no way round this and anyway it's part of their charm.

Bake for 20–25 minutes. This combination of nuts and flours takes a little longer to cook than the others. Once they are golden brown remove from the oven. If the outside crackers are browner remove these first and return the others to the oven for a further 5 or so minutes. Use a palette knife or similar to ease them apart and place on a cooling rack.

Once cool store in an airtight container. They keep for several weeks, provided the container is airtight.

Makes 12

- 100 g fine polenta
- 100 g gram flour
- 1 egg
- 50 g butter
- 2 tsp gluten free baking powder
- 250 g Greek yoghurt
- 50 g good blue cheese such as stilton or gorgonzola
- Pinch of salt
- 1 tsp glycerin

Preheat your oven to 180˚C.

Line a muffin tin with approx 15 cm squares of baking parchment. Don't be tempted to use fairy-cake cups: half the muffin peels off with the casing.

Melt the butter over a low heat and leave to cool. Put the polenta in a mixing bowl and sift the gram flour into it along with the baking powder (this is important because gram flour clumps and you will end up with lumps if you don't sift). Add the salt and stir them together. Add the yoghurt and mix thoroughly with a fork.

In a separate bowl beat the egg and add the cooled butter, mixing well. Add to the other ingredients and mix thoroughly.

Divide the mixture between the cases. Bake in the oven for 15 minutes. Test they are done by inserting a skewer, if it comes out clean they are done.

They are best eaten fresh from the oven, but will keep for three to four days in an airtight container. You can freeze them although they will be slightly more crumbly. I suggest that you only defrost what you think you will use on a given day.

The cottage cheese in this recipe gives a slightly sour flavour to the muffins similar to a sourdough loaf. The courgette and glycerine help to keep these muffins moist.

Makes 12

- 100 g fine polenta
- 100 g gram flour
- 1 egg
- 50 g butter
- 100 ml milk
- 250 g cottage cheese
- 1 medium sized courgette, about 120 g, grated
- 2 tsp gluten free baking powder
- 1 tsp glycerin
- 1 tsp paprika
- 1 tsp salt

Preheat your oven to 180°C. Line a muffin tin with approx 15 cm squares of baking parchment. Don't be tempted to use fairy-cake cups: half the muffin peels off with the casing.

Melt the butter over a low heat and leave to cool.

Put the polenta in a mixing bowl and sift the gram flour into it along with the baking powder and paprika (this is important because gram flour clumps and you will end up with lumps if you don't sift it). Add the salt and stir it all together.

In a separate bowl beat the egg and add the cottage cheese, milk, cooled butter and glycerin, mixing well. Add the wet ingredients and the grated courgette to the dry and mix thoroughly.

Divide the mixture between the cases. Bake in the oven for 20 minutes, and then turn it down to 150°C and bake for a further 5 minutes.

Test they are done by inserting a skewer, if it comes out clean they are done.

They are best eaten fresh from the oven, but will keep for three to four days in an airtight container. You can freeze them although they will be slightly more crumbly. I suggest that you only defrost what you think you will use on a given day.

Potatoes are used here to bind the flours together. You need to use a really floury potato such as Kerr's Pink or Cara. I use a sharp cheddar called Keens but use whatever you like and can find. You need very little salt because of the cheese.

- 500 g floury potatoes
- 75 g gram flour
- 75 g brown rice flour
- 50 g olive oil spread
- 50 g cheddar cheese
- 3 tsp gluten free baking powder
- 1 tsp paprika
- A pinch of salt

Peel the potatoes, cut into smallish pieces and boil until tender. Don't worry if they are starting to disintegrate. Drain, mash thoroughly and allow to cool.

Preheat your oven to 220˚C.

Grate the cheese. Sift the flours with the baking powder and paprika into a large bowl. Rub in the olive oil spread until it looks like breadcrumbs. Add a pinch of salt and the cheese and mix well.

Add the mashed potato to the bowl and, using a sturdy fork, mix everything together ensuring you have combined all the flour mix into the potato. It should all come together in a ball.

Line a large baking sheet with baking parchment.

Now divide your mix into 12 roughly equal parts and shape them into slightly flattened rounds. Put them on the baking sheet and place on a shelf in the top half of the oven. Cook for 10–15 minutes until golden and slightly risen.

As soon as they are cool enough to handle slather with butter and consume. Because of the potato they do remain fresh for a couple of days. You can also freeze them.

Chapter 4

~~~~~~~~~~

Small Savouries

Onion Bhajis (Vg)

Onion bhajis are a question of mind over matter. How on earth will they hold together in the oil? But they do. You just have to be brave. Every time you make them. But they are completely worth it. The first time I made onion bhajis I researched recipes on the internet and used one which a food writer had compiled after talking to top Indian chefs all of whose recipes were slightly different. All the schools in East Oxford which I worked in have wonderfully ethnically diverse populations. Whenever there was a bring-and-share lunch you could guarantee someone would bring onion bhajis. So when I made my own I knew what I expected to taste. But they didn't taste like those homemade ones I loved. The second time I made them I did them from memory and accidentally left out two of the ingredients. And this time they tasted as I had originally expected. So you see, making a mistake can lead you to a better dish.

Makes 8

- 60 g gram flour
- 30 g rice flour
- 2 medium sized onions, halved and thinly sliced
- 1 tbsp ghee or butter, melted
- 1 generous tbsp of lemon juice
- ½ tsp turmeric
- 1 tsp cumin seeds, coarsely chopped
- ¼ tsp fennel seeds
- 2 tsp root ginger, finely grated
- 2 cloves of garlic, finely chopped
- Several dried curry leaves, chopped
- Pinch of salt
- Vegetable oil, to cook

Separate out the onion slices so they don't stick to each other.

Sift the flours into a mixing bowl (this is important because gram flour clumps and you will end up with lumps if you don't sift), then stir in the ghee or butter and lemon juice and just enough cold water (about 70 ml) to bring it to the consistency of double cream. Stir in the spices, aromatics and herbs and add salt to taste. Stir in the onions so they are well coated.

Heat the oil in a deep-fat fryer, or fill a large pan a third full with oil and heat to 180°C – I use a cast iron saucepan. It is worth investing in a cooking thermometer: if the oil is too cold they won't cook and hold together, if the oil is too hot they will cook on the outside and be gooey inside. A drop of batter should sizzle as it hits the oil then float.

Meanwhile put a bowl of cold water by your pan and a plate lined with kitchen paper by the side of the stove. Put the oven on a low heat.

Once the oil is up to temperature, wet your hands and shape tablespoon-sized amounts of the mixture into balls. Drop into the oil, being careful not to overcrowd the pan, then stir carefully to stop them sticking. Wet your hands between each batch: it makes it easier to handle the batter.

Cook for about 10 minutes, turning occasionally, until crisp and golden, then drain on a plate lined with kitchen paper and put in the oven to keep warm while you cook the next batch. Serve with chutney or pickle. The yoghurt dip on *page 93* is very good with them.

These croquettes can be frozen before cooking and baked from frozen, so make a good 'store cupboard' food in your freezer for a quick meal when you don't have much time. Layer them in a container, placing pieces of baking parchment between each layer to prevent them from sticking together. They can also be frozen after cooking. You can warm them through from frozen in an oven at 150°C for about 10 minutes.

- 250 g almonds
- 125 g floury potatoes, boiled and mashed
- 100 g halloumi, grated
- 1 egg yolk, beaten (if you are doubling the recipe use 1 whole egg)
- 1 onion, finely chopped
- 2 cloves of garlic finely chopped
- Approx 50 g tomato paste
- 1–2 tsp dried oregano
- Sea salt
- Ground black pepper
- 2 tbsp olive oil

Preheat the oven to 180°C.

Place the olive oil in a frying pan and heat. Add the onions and fry over a low heat until they are softened but not browned. Add the garlic and cook for another 1–2 minutes.

Put the almonds in a food processor and crush until they are the texture of fine breadcrumbs. You are not aiming for flour.

Put the nuts, mashed potato and halloumi in a large bowl and mix until combined well. Add the onions and garlic, tomato paste and oregano, mix again and taste. Add salt and pepper to taste. When you are happy with the balance, add the egg and bring the mixture together to a dough.

Form into croquettes, approximately the size of a large walnut. Place them on a greased baking sheet and bake for approximately 10 minutes.

Serve with rice and Courgettes with Tomatoes and Cumin *(see on page 106)* or Green Beans with Onion and Tomato *(see on page 110)*.

Courgette Kofte (Vg)

People will tell you that courgettes are horribly watery and taste of nothing. They just don't know how to cook them. The texture of these is somewhere between an omelette and a pancake. The recipe is based on one from Madhur Jaffrey's *Eastern Vegetarian Cooking* and I have been making them for years.

Makes about 15

- *500 g courgettes*
- *2 medium onions*
- *1.5 cm cube of fresh ginger, finely grated*
- *2 chillies*
- *½ a large bunch of fresh coriander (I'm thinking of the large bunches we buy in the Crown Stores on Cowley Road. If you're buying from a supermarket use the whole lot.)*
- *45 g gram flour*
- *½ tsp salt*

Sunflower oil for cooking

Grate the courgettes or shred in a blender. Place in a colander over a deep bowl, sprinkle over the salt and mix it into the courgettes. Leave for at least half an hour, to extract as much moisture as possible. Put the salted courgettes into an old tea towel and squeeze out as much moisture as you can, into the bowl. You can use the juice as vegetable stock.

Finely chop or grate the onions (I use a food processor), finely chop the coriander and chilli and add to the onions along with the ginger. Tip into a large bowl.

Add courgettes, then sieve over the gram flour and mix thoroughly. Form into small balls the size of a walnut.

Heat 2 cm of sunflower oil in a heavy frying pan. When it is hot put a few of the balls in at a time and fry for 2–3 minutes. When the bottom is golden brown, turn to crisp the top. Remove from pan and put on a plate lined with kitchen paper to drain. I use a fish slice and a palette knife when turning them, otherwise it can be a bit fiddly.

I tend to make double quantities when we get a glut of courgettes and freeze them. Then you have 'instant' meals when you need them. They are very good with flatbreads and a spicy chutney.

- 225 g split red lentils
- 400 ml water
- 1 onion, finely chopped
- 4 cloves of garlic, finely chopped
- 2 tsp ground cumin
- 2 tsp ground coriander
- 1 tsp turmeric
- 2 chillies, finely chopped
- A rough 2 cm cube of fresh ginger, finely grated
- Zest of ½ a lime
- Juice of 1 lime
- 1 egg, beaten
- Sea salt and ground black pepper to taste
- 2 tbsp of olive oil
- Gram flour
- Sunflower oil for frying

Put the lentils and water in a large pot and bring to the boil. Lower the heat and simmer until the lentils have turned pale and all the water has been absorbed (about 30 minutes). Keep an eye on them and stir occasionally towards the end to prevent the lentils from sticking to the bottom of the pan.

Heat the oil in a frying pan and when hot add the onions. Cook on a low heat until the onions are soft but not browned. Add the garlic, ginger and chillies and cook for 2 minutes. Add the cumin and turmeric and cook for a further 2–3 minutes stirring the mixture.

Add the mixture to the lentils along with the fresh coriander, lime juice and zest. Add salt and pepper to taste. When you are satisfied with the balance of flavours, add the egg whilst the lentils are still warm and stir well. Leave the mixture to cool and then transfer to the fridge for at least an hour (you can leave it overnight if you wish) to firm up.

Sift a few tablespoons of gram flour in a shallow bowl or plate. Sift some more flour onto a large plate.

Form the lentil mixture into small cakes about 3 cm in diameter and 2 cm deep. Coat them in the gram flour and put them on the large plate.

When they are all done, put enough oil in a cast iron frying pan to fill it to a depth of approximately 1.5 cm. When the oil is good and hot, carefully place the cakes in the pan in batches and fry until golden brown. Carefully turn them over to fry on the other side. When they are done put them on a plate lined with kitchen paper to cool.

These cakes can be frozen, so you can take out however many you need to make a meal and leave the rest frozen. Layer them in a container, placing pieces of baking parchment between each layer to prevent them from sticking together.

It took me 30 years to work out how to make falafel. The main thing is, and I cannot emphasise this too strongly, do not, I repeat **do not** use tinned chickpeas. They must be dried: the cooking takes place when you fry them in the oil. You have been warned.

Now clearly you don't have to make sufficient to feed a small army, but this makes a good quantity for a party or as part of a mezze for a meal with family or friends. And they freeze well, meaning an 'instant' meal if you don't have much time. However, by all means halve the quantities.

Makes about 40

- 500 g dried chickpeas
- 80 g sesame seeds
- 2 onions, finely chopped
- ½ bulb garlic, cloves peeled and finely chopped
- 4 tsp ground cumin
- 4 tsp ground coriander
- 1 tsp cayenne peppe
- 1 tsp ground black pepper
- 1 tsp ground cardamom
- 2 tsp salt
- ½ tsp gluten free baking powder
- 90–100 g gram flour
- Vegetable oil

Put the chickpeas in a bowl and cover with water by about 5 cm. Leave for 24 hours or overnight. Drain and rinse and leave in a colander to dry off.

Finely chop the onion and garlic.

Put the chickpeas in the large bowl of a food processor with the onion, garlic, all the spices, salt and baking powder. Pulse the mixture until it resembles fine breadcrumbs. Pulsing rather than putting it on continuous mode will enable you to keep a check on the texture; you don't want a paste. Keep scraping the mixture down from the sides to ensure a reasonably uniform texture.

Put the mixture in a large bowl and leave it to rest for 1–2 hours.

Add the sesame seeds, sift over the flour and mix well. Take walnut sized pieces of the mix and press into rough spheres. Leave the falafel to rest for at least 15 minutes.

Heat the vegetable oil in a deep saucepan (I use a cast iron pan which works well). Obviously if you have a deep fat fryer you can use that. You will need a depth of approx 10–12 cm. Once the oil is very hot (test by putting a small amount of the mixture into the pot: it will sink to the bottom; once it rises to the surface and fizzes the oil is ready) using a slotted spoon place a few falafel into the pot and leave to cook. Don't overcrowd the pan. I do 5–6 at a time. They will take about 5–6 minutes each. Once golden brown remove with the slotted spoon and put on a plate lined with kitchen paper to drain.

The original recipe for this is from Madhur Jaffrey's *Eastern Vegetarian Cooking* and uses breadcrumbs for the crust. Polenta makes an excellent substitute.

For the potatoes

- *1 kg floury potatoes*
- *1 tsp salt*
- *Freshly ground black pepper*
- *¼ tsp cayenne pepper*

For the stuffing

- *180 g peas*
- *2 tbsp finely chopped fresh coriander*
- *½ tsp salt*
- *½ tsp ground cumin*

- *½ tsp ground coriander*
- *¼ tsp cayenne pepper*
- *Freshly ground black pepper*
- *Juice of half a lemon*

For the crust

- 100 g coarse polenta
- 1 tsp salt
- 1 tsp ground cumin
- 1 tsp ground turmeric
- ¼ tsp cayenne pepper
- ¼ tsp pepper
- 1 egg
- Gram flour for coating
- Vegetable oil for frying

Cook the potatoes and mash with the salt, pepper and cayenne. I don't peel my potatoes and I include the skin in the mash, but peel or remove the skins once cooked if you prefer. When the mash has cooled, divide it into 20 roughly equal patties.

You can use fresh or frozen peas. Cook them until tender. Combine with the other ingredients for the filling and lightly mash.

Whisk the egg in a small bowl. Combine the polenta and spices and put in another bowl. Sift some gram flour into a third bowl.

Take one of the patties in the palm of one hand and using your other thumb press the potato into a nest into which you can put your filling. Put 1–2 teaspoons of the filling in the nest and squeeze the potato around the filling to enclose it completely. Do the same for each patty.

Taking each patty in turn coat it in gram flour, dip in the egg and then into the polenta mix.

In a heavy frying pan pour 2 cm depth of vegetable oil and heat. Test by dropping a bit of the crust into it. If it fizzes it's ready. Put the patties in the pan and cook until golden, turn them over to cook the other side. Don't overcrowd the pan. Remove with a fish slice and put on a plate lined with kitchen paper so they can cool.

Serves 2-3 as a main or 4-6 as a side dish.

The whole spices used in this dish make it a very mild but fragrant curry. If you don't have any homemade tomato sauce hanging around in the freezer you can use a jar of passata or blitz a tin of tomatoes. Anardana are dried pomegranate seeds. You can get them in Asian stores and they provide a sour note. If you cannot get hold of them add another tablespoon of lime or lemon juice. You could omit the yoghurt to make this dish suitable for vegans

- *2 medium sized squash*
- *4 onions*
- *2 cloves of garlic*
- *400 ml homemade tomato sauce*
- *200 ml coconut milk*
- *2 tbsps olive oil*
- *1 stick cinnamon*
- *10 green cardamom pods*
- *15 black peppercorns*
- *15 whole cloves*
- *1 tsp cumin seeds*
- *2 tsp anardana*
- *2 bay leaves*
- *1 tbsp tomato paste*
- *Juice of 1 lime*
- *50 ml yoghurt*
- *15 g flaked almonds*
- *Salt*
- *Ground black pepper*

Preheat your oven to 180°C

Cut the squash in half and remove the seeds and the stringy fresh around them. Cut into wedges. Peel the wedges and cut into largish chunks. Pour a tablespoon of olive oil over the base of a large baking tray and arrange the squash in the tray. Pour over another tbsp of olive oil. Cook for approximately 30 minutes until the edges of the squash begin to blacken and caramelize and the squash feels soft when a knife is inserted. Leave to cool.

Peel and roughly chop the onions. Peel and finely chop the garlic. Heat the olive oil in a large heavy casserole. Put in the cinnamon, cardamom, peppercorns, cloves, cumin seeds, anardana (if using) and the bay leaves. Allow them to cook in the oil for 2 minutes before adding the onions, with a pinch of salt. Turn the heat down to the lowest setting and cook until the onions are soft. Add the garlic and cook for a further 2–3 minutes. Add the tomato paste and combine thoroughly with the onions. Pour in the tomato sauce and coconut milk, bring to the boil then reduce the heat and simmer uncovered for 15 minutes. The sauce should have reduced and thickened.

Meanwhile cut the cooled chunks of squash into rough 1 cm cubes. Add to the sauce together with the lime juice and a teaspoon of salt. Taste. Add more salt if you think it needs it. Cover the pot and simmer for a further 15 minutes. Stir occasionally to ensure it is not sticking.

In a small pan heat a teaspoon of olive oil and toast the flaked almonds until they are golden. Remove the curry from the heat and stir in the almonds and yoghurt.

Serve on its own with rice and/or Indian flatbreads as a main dish, or with rice and courgette kofte or almond croquettes as a side dish.

Chickpea Dal (Vg)

This is based on Madhur Jaffrey's recipe for chana masaledar a in *An Invitation to Indian Cooking*. My copy dates from 1981 and is dog-eared and food stained. The original includes garam marsala for which I have substituted ground cumin because I prefer it. The choice of spice is yours.

- 1 tin of chickpeas 400 g
- 1 medium onion
- 2 cloves of garlic
- 1.5 cm cube fresh ginger
- 1 tbsp tomato purée
- ¼ tsp cumin seeds
- 1 tsp ground cumin
- 1 tsp ground coriander
- Pinch of cayenne pepper
- 1 tsp of amchoor or the juice of half a lemon
- 3-4 tbsp olive oil
- Salt to taste

Serves 2 as a main or 4 as a side dish.

Drain the chickpeas over a bowl. Retain 150 ml of the liquid. Peel and chop the onions. Peel and finely chop the garlic. Peel and grate the ginger.

Heat a couple of tablespoons of olive oil in a small casserole or heavy saucepan. Add the cumin seeds. When they start to darken add the onions and turn the heat to low. Cook for approximately 5 minutes until the onions have softened.

Add the cumin and coriander and mix in thoroughly, then add the garlic and ginger and cook for a couple of minutes. Add the tomato purée and mix in thoroughly, then add the chickpeas, the chickpea liquid, the cayenne, lemon juice and ½ tsp of salt. Mix thoroughly, then cover and cook over a low heat for approximately 30 minutes. Serve with rice or flatbreads.

Winter Squash and Lentil Soup (Vg)

You can use any winter squash for this soup. Butternuts are the most readily available, but seek out others in small shops and farmers' markets. My partner Roy grows lots of different sorts, many from saved seed so you are never quite sure what you are going to get.

To shred the squash cut it in half and remove the seeds and the stringy fresh around them. Cut into wedges and peel. Grate the wedges or use a food processor to shred the squash. Alternatively chop finely.

It is very important to use unsalted stock, so don't be tempted to use a commercial stock cube. If you cook any pulse in salted water it will be tough and unpleasant. You add the salt right at the end. If you don't have any homemade stock use water.

- 400 g shredded winter squash
- 100 g split red lentils
- 800 ml unsalted vegetable stock or water
- 300–400 g tomato pulp or sauce
- 2 onions, roughly chopped
- 3–4 cloves of garlic, chopped
- 1 tsp of grated fresh ginger – a piece approximately 2 cm cubed
- 2 tsp ground cumin
- 1 small chilli, seeded and finely chopped
- 1 tsp paprika
- 2 tsp salt
- Juice of 1 lime
- Olive oil

In a large saucepan or stockpot heat a couple of tablespoons of olive oil and cook the onions with a pinch of salt on a very low heat until softened – about 10 minutes. Stir frequently. Add the garlic, ginger and chilli and cook for a couple of minutes before adding the cumin and paprika. Cook for another couple of minutes stirring frequently. Add the squash and lentils and stir well before adding the stock, water if using, and tomato. Stir well and bring the soup to the boil, before turning down the heat to simmer for 30–40 minutes until the lentils are cooked. Add the salt and lime juice, tasting to ensure the right salt/sour balance. Cook for a couple of minutes more then turn off the heat. Blend with a stick blender.

This soup is nice with Indian flatbreads.

This is a dish for cold autumn and winter days. I adapted it from one in *The Mushroom Book* by Thomas Loessoe and Anna Pavord a few years ago when we bought a Mont D'Or cheese in the Saint-Quentin Market in Paris on the way home from somewhere. We did not realise that it was for making raclette or that it was alive and possibly had the ability to walk. It is wonderfully smelly and unctuous, but you could substitute fontina, taleggio or good old feta if you prefer. Use any combination of mushrooms you want or just one sort. Chestnut, portobello, shitake and oyster all work well, as do ordinary button mushrooms. I used polenta with truffle in it, because my friend Joan had brought me back a packet from Italy, but ordinary polenta works just as well.

- 400 g polenta with or without truffle
- 2.5 litres water
- 450 g mixed mushrooms
- 500 g Mont D'Or cheese
- 50 g butter
- 50 g gram flour
- 750 ml whole milk
- Salt and pepper

Preheat the oven to 200°C.

First make the polenta. Salt the water and bring to the boil. Pour in the polenta in a stream stirring with a wooden spoon all the while and keep beating as you cook it. Once it has become a stiff paste remove from the heat and pour it into a well buttered shallow ovenproof dish.

Cover with buttered aluminium foil and bake for one hour. Leave to cool.

Clean and slice the mushrooms. It looks like a huge amount but they do cook down.

Heat the butter in a large saucepan. Add the mushrooms to the pan with a couple of large pinches of salt. Cook, stirring occasionally, until they are completely tender. Sift in the gram flour and stir well with a wooden spoon to make a roux. Add the milk gradually and keep stirring until you have a thick béchamel mushroom sauce.

Preheat the oven to 180°C. Slice the cooled polenta and the cheese. Butter a large shallow ovenproof dish. Start with a layer of the mushroom sauce on the bottom, followed by a layer of polenta and then a layer of cheese. Repeat until all the ingredients are used up, finishing with a layer of cheese.

Bake for 30 minutes. It will be bubbling and practically alive when you remove it from the oven, so it is best to let it stand for a few minutes before serving.

Many years ago I read a piece by Richard Erlich in the Saturday *Guardian* magazine. He advised that if you bought just one book on Italian cooking it should be Anna Del Conte's *The Gastronomy of Italy*. I duly visited a local bookshop and bought it (mine is a lovely hard-backed version). I have never regretted the purchase: every recipe is a gem. This recipe is based on her version of this dish from that book. I use fresh tomatoes, but you can equally well use tinned (a 400 g tin) as in the original recipe, or you can use passata (400 ml).

Some recipes include the use of breadcrumbs to line the dish, add a crunchy topping, or coat the individual aubergine slices, others dredge the slices in egg and flour. None of this is necessary and leaving them out, as Anna Del Conte does, in no way detracts from the overall taste of the dish.

I love aubergines, and this is probably my favourite aubergine dish. If I see it on the menu of an Italian restaurant I, like my sister-in-law Sue, will always order it, provided of course that it contains no breadcrumbs.

Serves 4

- 600–700 g aubergines
- 400 g tomatoes
- 2 balls of fresh mozzarella (approximately 250 g)
- 50 g parmesan
- 2 hardboiled eggs
- 1 clove garlic
- 1 small handful of basil leaves
- Olive oil
- Vegetable oil

Slice the aubergines lengthways into 5 mm thick slices. Put in a colander and salt liberally. Leave for at least an hour. Then rinse under the cold tap and pat dry. I do this by laying them on a clean tea towel, then covering with another tea towel and leaving them for 5–10 minutes.

In the meantime skin the tomatoes if you are using fresh. Place them in a bowl and pour over boiling water. Leave for 2 minutes, then drain and cover with cold water to stop the cooking process. Skin, core and chop.

Crush the garlic with the back of a knife so it is bruised but remains whole. Put 2 tbsp of olive oil in a saucepan or small casserole and add the tomatoes, garlic, and torn basil leaves. Bring to a simmer and cook over a low heat for approximately 10 minutes. Blend using a stick blender, food processor or food mill.

Pour vegetable oil into a heavy frying pan or casserole (I use my large Le Creuset casserole) to a depth of 2 cm and bring to heat. It is ready when, if you dip in the end of a piece of aubergine, it sizzles. Put pieces of aubergine into the oil, in a single layer and cook until golden. Remove with a slotted spoon and place on a plate covered with kitchen paper, to drain. Continue with the remaining pieces.

Preheat your oven to 170°C.

Slice the eggs and mozzarella, grate the parmesan.

Brush the base of an ovenproof dish with a tsp olive oil. Put a single layer of aubergine in the bottom of a casserole dish. Cover with a thin layer of sauce, then cover with a layer of egg and mozzarella, and sprinkle over some parmesan. Keep about half of the parmesan for the final layer if you like a nice cheesy topping. Continue with the layers, finishing with a layer of aubergines covered with the remaining parmesan.

Cook for 30 minutes. Leave to cool for at least 10 minutes and up to half an hour.

Matthew Fort's Mum's Roasted Almonds (Vg)

This is another recipe from a newspaper cutting of yesteryear. They were apparently his mother's Christmas speciality. And jolly good they are too. I make them twice a year, once at Christmas and in August for our annual party. You can buy large bags of raw almonds in Asian and Middle Eastern shops relatively cheaply.

- 450–500 g raw almonds in their skins
- Olive oil
- Salt
- Cayenne pepper

Blanch the almonds in boiling water for two minutes, then drain. Rub off the skins. I spread a tea towel on the dining table and take the bowl of almonds plus two others, one for the skins, one for the peeled almonds, along with a cup of tea. I sit down for this operation which takes a little time.

Lay the peeled almonds out on two large baking trays, somewhere warm, to completely dry off. I leave them overnight.

Preheat your oven to 135°C. Drizzle a little olive oil over the almonds and roll them around in it to ensure they are well covered. Place in the oven and cook for 25-30 minutes. They should be golden brown. Leave to cool on the trays.

Line an airtight plastic tub or wide necked jar with greaseproof paper. Tip the cooled almonds into the container and sprinkle liberally with salt. Put the lid on.

When you are ready to use them balance a colander over the sink and tip the salted almonds into it. Shake off the excess salt, dispose of the greaseproof paper, and put the almonds back in the container. Sprinkle over a little cayenne pepper, and shake the container to distribute the pepper over the almonds.

Serve in small dishes with a glass of prosecco or wine – or any other tipple of your choice.

Chapter 5

Vegetables & Salads

We have two allotments. My partner Roy works them. We started out with one and worked it together. We talked about getting a second one once we sorted out the first one. About a year after we'd started allotmenteering Roy came home one day and announced we had a second plot. I was not pleased, and I sort of lost interest. Now Roy works the allotments mostly and I am in charge of the garden mostly. It works fine.

Courgettes absorb flavour really well. Making a flavoursome tomato sauce and then cooking the courgettes in it results in a really delicious dish. I sometimes make this out of tomato season if the courgettes start cropping early and heavily before the tomatoes are on stream, as happened in 2017, using last year's homemade tomato sauce from the freezer. If you want to do this you need approximately 250 ml of sauce. You could also use tinned tomatoes. This is a great dish for a courgette glut, and freezes well.

- *250 g courgettes*
- *500 g tomatoes*
- *2 medium onions*
- *1 tsp cumin seeds*
- *2 dried chillies*
- *Large pinch of ground black pepper*
- *1 tsp salt*
- *Juice of ½ lemon*
- *2 tbsp olive oil*

Cut the onions in half-length ways and the slice into half-moons. Cut the courgettes into 1 cm thick slices.

Cover the tomatoes with boiling water and leave for 2 minutes. Drain and cover with cold water to stop them cooking further. Peel and chop.

Heat the olive oil in a small casserole. Put in the cumin seeds, once they start to darken add the onions, sprinkle with a little salt, and cook over a low heat for approximately 5 minutes.

Add the tomatoes, the courgettes, dried chillies and salt, put the lid on the pan and cook on a medium heat for 20 minutes or until the courgettes have begun to soften, stirring occasionally to ensure all the courgettes cook in the tomato sauce. Remove the lid and cook uncovered for a further 10–20 minutes. Make sure all the courgettes have softened.

Add the lemon juice and pepper, stir and cook for a further minute. Taste, checking for a salt sour balance. Remove the chillies before serving.

This dish can be served hot or at room temperature. It makes an excellent accompaniment to falafel or lentil cakes served with flatbreads or rice.

A khoreshe is a Persian sauce to be served with rice. I have been making this dish since the 1980s. The recipe is based on one from David Scott's *Middle Eastern Vegetarian Cookery*. It is aromatic with the spices and sour with the lemon juice. The onion garnish adds another texture.

- 400 g tomatoes
- 2 medium onions
- 150 g green peppers, 1 large or 2 small
- 2 medium courgettes, approximately 200 g
- 1 lemon
- 1 tsp cinnamon
- ½ tsp pimento or paprika
- ¼ tsp turmeric
- ¼ tsp ground nutmeg
- 1 clove of garlic
- 1 tbsp of fresh mint
- Salt and pepper to taste
- 3–4 tbsp olive oil

Cover the tomatoes with boiling water and leave for 2 minutes. Drain and cover with cold water to stop them cooking further. Peel and chop.

Peel and slice the onions. Cut the peppers in half, remove the seeds and pith. Cut them into strips. Slice the courgettes into 3 mm slices. Juice the lemon.

Heat some olive oil in a small casserole or medium saucepan. Add the courgettes and three quarters of the onions and cook over a low heat until softened. Add the peppers, tomatoes, lemon juice and the spices. Bring to the boil, then reduce the heat, and simmer for 30 minutes until all the vegetables are soft and the liquid has reduced, stirring occasionally. If it dries out too much add a little water.

Peel and finely chop the garlic. Chop the mint.

In a small pan heat a small amount of olive oil and add the remaining onion. Once they have softened and are going brown in spots, add the garlic and mint and cook for a further 2–3 minutes.

Garnish the khoreshe with the onion mixture and serve with rice.

This is a Lebanese dish called Loubia bi zeit. My version is adapted from Claudia Roden's version in *A New Book of Middle Eastern Food*. I added the cinnamon after I tasted it in a version I ate in the wonderful Pomegranate restaurant on the Cowley Road. You can also make it using tinned tomatoes or passata. If you are using the latter you will need to cook the beans covered.

- 500 g French beans
- 500 g tomatoes
- 1 large or 2 medium onions
- 4 cloves garlic

- 4–5 tbsp olive oil
- ½ tsp cinnamon
- ½ tsp pepper
- ½ tsp salt

Peel and roughly chop the onion.

Heat the oil in a small casserole or large frying pan with a lid, on a low heat. Add the onion and sprinkle a little salt over it. Cook on a low heat until the onion softens, about 5 minutes.

Peel and finely chop the garlic, add to the pan and cook for 2 minutes stirring frequently.

Put the tomatoes in a bowl and cover with boiling water for 2 minutes. Drain and cover with cold water. When they are cool enough to handle (1–2 minutes) peel them, remove the tough parts of the core and chop. Add to the pan with the salt and pepper, cover and, still on the lowest heat possible, cook for 10 minutes. If the mixture gets too dry add a little water. If you are using passata you do not need to cook the sauce.

Meanwhile top and tail the beans and chop into 2–3 cm pieces. Add the beans to the tomato and mix well.

Cook uncovered for 15–20 minutes (covered if you are using passata) or until the beans have softened, making sure the mixture does not dry out.

Add the salt and pepper, taste and adjust seasoning as necessary. The dish can be served hot or at room temperature.

Serves 4-6 depending on how much you love your beans.

I don't like runner beans, they so quickly get stringy and indigestible. But I love French beans and my partner Roy grows lots of them. If you prefer runner beans you could of course substitute them. I use unsalted butter but if you use salted then omit the salt from the recipe

- 300 g French Beans topped & tailed
- 25 g unsalted butter
- Juice of half a lemon
- Salt
- Pepper

Boil the beans in salted water until tender.

In the meantime melt the butter in a separate pan with a pinch of salt and pepper. Add the lemon juice and mix well.

Tip the cooked beans into the sauce and make sure they are well coated. These are lovely with the courgette tart or lentil cakes.

Roast Squash With Fennel Seeds

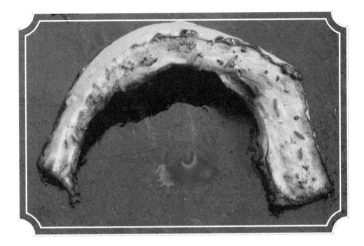

You need a smallish squash for this recipe. It is very easy to prepare.

- *1 small squash*
- *1 tbsp olive oil*
- *½ tsp salt*
- *½ tsp pepper*
- *½ tsp fennel seeds*

Preheat the oven to 160°C.

Cut the squash in half and remove the seeds and the stringy fresh around them. Cut into wedges.

Oil a metal tray or ceramic baking dish with 1-2 tsp of olive oil. Place the squash wedges in the pan and drizzle more olive oil over them. You just need enough to make sure both sides of the wedge are coated.

Sprinkle the salt and pepper over them and then the fennel seeds, making sure as many of the seeds as possible adhere to the squash and don't fall into the pan.

Cook in the oven for approximately 20 minutes, checking from time to time. Serves 4–6. The squash is very nice with a vegetable tart or kofte.

This is based on a Lebanese recipe from Claudia Roden's *Arabesque*. The original contains fresh coriander and garlic, which is lovely, but I find this simplified version more versatile.

Serves 4–6 as part of a mezze or as a side dish.

- *1 kg of potatoes, a salad variety such as Pink Fir Apple or Charlotte is perfect*
- *Olive oil*
- *Juice of a large lemon*
- *Salt and black pepper*

I don't peel my potatoes but you can if you wish. Well I can't stop you can I? Cut into smallish pieces and parboil for approximately 10 minutes. Drain and leave to cool.

Preheat your oven to 230°C.

Drizzle some olive oil in a large roasting tin. Once the potatoes are cool enough to handle, cut them into small cubes, approximately 1.5 cm. Tip them into the roasting tin in a single layer and drizzle a little more olive oil over them, then sprinkle with salt and pepper. Cook in the oven for about 30 minutes. The potatoes should be golden and crisp.

Put the potatoes in a warmed serving dish and pour over the lemon juice. Serve immediately.

People turn their noses up at vegetables like cabbage and kale. You just have to know how to cook them. In *The Vegetarian Epicure* Anna Thomas has a recipe for a Russian Vegetable Pie which contains cabbage, well of course it does. But first the cabbage is cooked in butter. This makes a slightly luxurious side dish.

If you don't have any fresh thyme use ¼–½ tsp of dried. Start with a little and add to taste. Dried thyme has a much stronger taste than fresh.

- *1 small head of cabbage*
- *1 medium sized onion*
- *2 sprigs of thyme*
- *30 g butter*
- *Salt and pepper*

Cut the cabbage in half and remove the course inner ribs. Coarsely shred the cabbage. Peel and slice the onion. Pick the leaves off the thyme and roughly chop.

In a saucepan melt the butter over a low heat. Once it has all melted add the cabbage and the onion and cook for about 5 minutes, stirring from time to time.

Add the thyme and continue cooking until the cabbage has wilted and the onion is soft. Season to taste. Serve immediately.

Fatoush is one of those peasant dishes of which there are as many versions as people who make it. Some add lettuce, preferably little gem, some add radishes, some use vinegar in the dressing. My version is based on Claudia Roden's recipe in *A New Book of Middle Eastern Food* and the one that is made in our local Lebanese restaurants.

- 2 basic flatbreads (see on page 40)
- 1 cucumber
- 4 largish tomatoes
- 1 red onion
- A bunch of parsley
- 2 tbsps fresh mint
- 2 cloves garlic
- Juice of 1–2 lemons
- 6–8 tbsps olive oil
- Salt and black pepper to taste
- 1 tsp sumac

Chop the garlic very finely and mix it with the oil and lemon, salt and pepper and leave to infuse.

Chop the cucumber and tomatoes into rough cubes of approximately 1 cm.

Dice the onion.

Roughly chop the mint and parsley, you want quite large pieces.

Tear the flatbread into rough pieces.

Combine the onion, tomatoes and cucumber with the herbs and dress with the oil and lemon, and season to taste.

Scatter the bread over the salad and then sprinkle with the sumac.

This is a simple but quite filling salad which makes an easy lunch with flatbreads. I fill the flatbreads, fold them over and munch. This results in dribbles down the chin and onto the plate. If you have more refined manners, you can eat the salad with a fork and use the flatbread to mop up the juices.

I got the idea for this from our friend Richard who prepared a dish of feta cheese, drizzled with lemon oil and oregano as part of a mezze style first course for a delicious summer lunch.

- 400 g tomatoes
- 200 g feta cheese
- Olive oil
- Pepper
- Oregano
- Lemon zest

Cut the tomatoes into rough 1 cm cubes. Cut the feta into similarly sized pieces. Mix together in a bowl. Drizzle with olive oil, add a pinch of pepper and the oregano. Zest approximately a quarter of a lemon over the mixture. Combine thoroughly. Simples.

Greek salad is another of those dishes which is basically a recipe which you vary with the season and what you have to hand. I have seen versions with potato in them. This is the version I make every year for our party. Sometimes at the end of summer when we harvest our first tomatoes and cucumbers are plentiful, I make a small quantity for lunch. In this case I use whatever olives we have. Then I pile it into flatbreads and eat them like a wrap. Serves 2–4 depending on whether you are serving it as a main meal or as a side-salad.

- *4 large tomatoes*
- *1 large cucumber*
- *½ a red onion*
- *12 Kalamata olives*
- *1 small green or red pepper*
- *1 200 g pack of feta cheese*
- *1 tbsp preserved capers*
- *Juice of ½ a lemon*
- *1 tbsp good olive oil*
- *1 tsp of dried oregano*
- *Black pepper*

Chop the tomatoes and cucumbers into largish chunks.

Chop the onion in half lengthways and then slice into half-moons.

If the olives are not pitted remove the stones.

Remove the stalk and seeds from the pepper along with any pith. Cut into strips lengthways and then cut the strips in half. Put a heavy frying pan on a high heat and, without any oil, dry fry the peppers until they have softened a little. Leave to cool.

Put the tomatoes and cucumbers in a bowl with the olives, onion and capers. Roughly crumble the feta cheese into the bowl. Pour over the olive oil and lemon juice and sprinkle in the pepper and oregano. Once cooled, add the peppers.

Mix it all together well and leave for at least half an hour to let the flavours mingle and oregano permeate the salad.

Serve with flatbreads or as part of a mezze.

Every year when the cucumbers become a glut I scour all my cookbooks to find recipes to use them up. And every year I come across a recipe which pairs cucumbers with peanuts either used raw or boiled, which apparently taste like chestnuts. I don't like chestnuts much and I think raw they would be too soft in a salad so every year I reject the recipe. Then I recently made an Olia Hercules recipe which uses roasted walnuts with tomatoes and cucumbers in a lovely herby salad. This recipe is what I believe the young people call a 'mashup' between those two recipes.

- 400 g cucumbers (approximately 2–3 small or one large)
- 1 small red onion
- 50 g raw peanuts
- 10 ml olive oil
- 10 ml white wine vinegar
- 10 ml runny honey
- Salt
- Cayenne pepper

Turn the oven to 150°C. Spread the peanuts in a single layer in a baking tray and place in the oven. Roast them for 10–15 minutes until they are golden. Leave them to cool and then rub off the skins. Place the skinned peanuts in a paper bag and crush a bit with a rolling pin or use the pulse setting on your food processor to break them up a bit.

If the skin of the cucumbers is very tough peel them. Chop them into roughly 1 cm cubes and place in a bowl.

Chop the onion quite finely and add to the bowl.

Mix the olive oil, white wine vinegar and honey together and season with salt and a pinch of cayenne pepper to taste. You want an underlying heat, not to blow your head off.

Add the peanuts to the cucumber and onion and dress.

Winter squash is very versatile but it is sweet so needs sharp and sour flavours to counter this. This is a salad for cold winter's day: stick to your ribs food. Make it fresh because the squash should still be warm.

If you prefer an English mustard then use that but check the contents carefully. Many contain gluten, whereas I have never found a jar of Dijon mustard that does. It is worth buying decent olives from a delicatessen rather than a jar of pitted olives, which often taste of nothing very much.

- 1 small winter squash
- 8 small salad potatoes such as Charlotte or Pink Fir Apple
- 200 g Feta cheese
- 3 eggs
- 4 small onions

- About 20 black olives
- 15 ml olive oil
- 15 ml cider vinegar
- 1 tsp Dijon mustard
- ¼ tsp paprika
- A pinch of salt

Preheat your oven to 200°C. Cut the squash in half and remove the seeds and the stringy fresh around them. Cut into wedges. Peel the wedges and cut into largish chunks. Peel the onions and remove the bases.

Take a large roasting tray and drizzle the bottom with a couple of tablespoons of olive oil. Arrange the squash and the onions in a single layer. Drizzle with a little more oil and sprinkle with salt and pepper. Roast for approximately 30 minutes until the squash are starting to darken at the edges. Remove from the oven and allow to cool.

Slice the potatoes in half and boil in salted water until tender. Drain and leave to cool.

Hard boil the eggs for approximately 5 minutes. Drain them and cover with cold water to prevent them cooking further. You will probably need to change the water once or twice. Once cool, peel and chop into largish chunks.

Cut the olives in half and remove the stones. Cut or break the feta cheese into rough 1.5 cm cubes.

Mix the olive oil, cider vinegar, mustard and paprika in a small bowl until the mustard is well incorporated with the other ingredients. Season to taste.

Cut the cooled squash, onions and potatoes into rough 1.5–2 cm cubes and place in a large serving bowl. Quarter the onions and add to the bowl. Add the eggs, cheese and olives. Dress and serve.

We eat industrial quantities of hummus in our house. The following recipe makes approximately 1400 g of the stuff. I keep one tub in the fridge and freeze the other two. The recipe is based partly on laziness. If I'm making one lot of hummus, as my friend Joan pointed out, why not make twice the amount and freeze half. Somehow when I double the recipe I end up with three times the amount. No, me neither.

Tahina separates somewhat in the tub and it is a faff to combine it well and measure out the requisite amount, and you end up wasting more than is strictly necessary. So what is the answer? Use the whole tub of course. Still messy, and some gets wasted but get as much out as you can with the aid of a rubber spoon and then lick the spoon.

- *2 x 400 g tins of chickpeas, drained, liquid retained*
- *1 450 g tub of tahina*
- *4–8 cloves garlic, depending on their size and your taste*
- *Juice of 2–3 lemons, depending on size*
- *200 ml of reserved liquid from the chickpeas*
- *2 tsp salt*
- *1 tsp freshly ground black pepper*

You need to start by draining the chickpeas over a bowl in order to retain the liquid (you won't need all of it).

Finely chop the garlic.

Place the chickpeas in a food processor with the tahina (yes, I thought it was tahini too but check the tubs and Claudia Roden, we were wrong) garlic and the juice from **two** of the lemons and blitz. The resulting paste will be stiff. Gradually add the liquid from the chickpeas to let down the mixture until it is the consistency of whipped double cream. Add salt, ½ tsp at a time, and pepper, mix again and taste. Add more lemon juice and salt to taste. You can keep adding more liquid if you think the mixture is too thick and if the chickpeas have not completely broken down. Once you are happy with the taste and consistency empty into containers.

For those of you who don't have a freezer, or are not as fond of hummus as I am, here are two recipes with rather more sensible quantities of ingredients.

These recipes are based on Claudia Roden's recipes from her *A New Book of Middle Eastern Food*. Hummus refers to the bean paste. Once you add tahina it is called Hummus bi tahina (version 3).

- *1 400 g tin of chickpeas*
- *3–4 cloves garlic, depending on their size and your taste*
- *Juice of 1 large lemon*
- *50 ml good olive oil*
- *1 tsp salt*
- *2 tsps ground cumin*
- *A good pinch of cayenne pepper*

Drain the chickpeas over a bowl and retain the liquid. Finely chop the garlic. Place the chickpeas in a food processor with the olive oil and lemon juice and blitz.

Add the garlic, cumin, cayenne and half the salt and, if you think it is too thick add some of the chickpea liquid, and blitz again. Taste and add more salt and/or lemon juice to taste.

- 1 400 g tin of chickpeas
- 150 ml tahina
- 3-4 cloves garlic, depending on their size and your taste
- Juice of 2 large lemons
- 1 tsp salt

Drain the chickpeas over a bowl and retain the liquid. Finely chop the garlic.

Place the chickpeas in a food processor with the tahina, garlic and the lemon juice and blitz. Add half the salt, mix again and taste.

Add more lemon juice and salt to taste.

You can keep adding more liquid if you think the mixture is too thick and if the chickpeas have not completely broken down. It should be the consistency of whipped cream.

Cannelini Bean Puree

This is a really quick purée to make and good with flatbreads, crackers or blini.

- 1 tin cannelini beans
- Juice of one lemon
- Salt
- Pepper
- 1 tsp dried oregano

Simply put all the ingredients in the small bowl of a food processor and blitz together. If you don't have a food processor, put them in a bowl and use a stick blender. Alternatively mash the beans with a fork or use a pestle and mortar and then stir the other ingredients in. Whichever method you chose it will only take minutes to make.

Tahina Salad

In the Middle East and Greece, salad covers cold pastes or dips such as hummus, cacik and taramasalata (yes I know it contains fish eggs; you don't have to eat it) as well as vegetable and fruit salads.

- *150 ml tahina*
- *150 ml lemon juice*
- *3–4 cloves of garlic*
- *2 tsp ground cumin*
- *1 tsp salt or to taste*

Beat the tahina and lemon juice together in a bowl. The mixture will at first appear to curdle but keep going and it comes together in a thick paste. Add the other ingredients. You can keep this in the fridge for a few days. It also freezes well. Serve with flatbreads or to dress a bean salad.

Simple Bean Salad with Tahina (Vg)

You can use any dried bean for this. I personally favour borlotti beans but cannellini, kidney or butter beans would work equally well. You can also use tinned beans, making it even simpler.

- *250 g borlotti beans*
- *250 g tomatoes*
- *1 quantity of tahina salad (see above)*
- *2 bay leaves*

Soak the beans in plenty of water overnight. Drain the beans and put them in a deep saucepan with plenty of unsalted water and a couple of bay leaves, bring to the boil and cook until tender (about an hour). Drain and leave to cool. Chop the tomatoes into rough 1 cm cubes. Mix the beans with the tomatoes and dress with the tahina salad.

This is based on a chutney recipe from Madhur Jaffrey's *An Invitation to Indian Cooking*. Use a good thick Greek or Turkish yoghurt.

- *500 ml Greek yoghurt*
- *½ tsp salt*
- *½ tsp cumin seeds*
- *Ground pepper*

- *Juice of ½ lemon*
- *1 fresh chilli, finely chopped*
- *1 large bunch coriander, finely chopped.*

Put the coriander and chilli in a blender or food processor (smallest bowl) with 4 tbsp of water and blend until you have a smooth paste. Add more water if the mixture seems dry.

Roast the cumin seeds in a small heavy pan and then grind with a pestle and mortar.

In a non-metallic bowl combine the yoghurt with the lemon juice, cumin and paste. Season to taste. Refrigerate until you are ready to use it. Serve with onion bhajis, samosas, lime and ginger lentil cakes or courgette kofte. You can make this the day before you want to use it, and it keeps for several days in the fridge.

There are variations of this across North Africa and Southern Europe. I had a version in Sicily with anchovies (I told you I wasn't a vegetarian). This is based on a recipe from Claudia Roden's wonderful *Arabesque*. It's a lovely dish to make in the winter with Seville oranges if you like bitterness or blood oranges if you prefer your oranges sweet.

- 4 seville or blood oranges
- 15 -20 black olives, pitted
- 1 red onion, finely chopped
- Juice of ½–1 lemon
- 3 tbsps olive oil
- 1 tsp cumin
- 1 tsp paprika
- Salt
- Pinch of cayenne pepper
- 1 bunch of flat-leaved parsley or fresh coriander, chopped

One bunch of flat-leaved parsley or fresh coriander, chopped

Peel the oranges removing as much pith as possible. Divide into individual segments and cut into 2 or 3 pieces. Place in a serving bowl and arrange the onion and olives on top.

Make the dressing with the oil and lemon, adding the cumin, paprika, salt and chilli. Mix well and pour over the salad. Dress with the chopped parsley.

This is based on a dal recipe from Madhur Jaffrey's *An Invitation to Indian Cooking*. You can use any waxy potato for these. A salad potato such as Pink Fir Apple works particularly well. I like the sharpness of lime juice but you could use the juice of half a lemon if you prefer.

- 500 g waxy potatoes
- 1 400 g tin of chickpeas, drained
- Juice of one lime
- 1 medium onion
- 4 tbsps sunflower oil
- 1.5 cm cubed piece of fresh ginger
- ½ tsp mustard seeds
- ½ tsp cumin seeds
- 15-20 fenugreek seeds
- 2 fresh green chillies or ¼ tsp cayenne pepper
- ½-1 tsp salt, to taste
- A pinch of ground black pepper

Cut the potato into smallish pieces and boil until tender. Drain and let them cool. Chop them into roughly 1 cm cubes.

Chop the onion. Peel and finely grate the ginger. Finely chop the chilli. It's up to you whether to include the seeds which increase the heat. I do because I like the heat, but omit them if you don't.

Heat the oil in a large frying pan or casserole dish on a low heat. When the oil is hot add the cumin, mustard and fenugreek seeds. When the mustard seeds start to pop add the onion, chilli and ginger and cook slowly until the onion has softened, stirring frequently.

Add the chickpeas, potatoes, salt, pepper and lime juice and mix well. Cook over a low heat for about 5 minutes stirring frequently.

This goes well with any of the kofte recipes.

Radish Salad With Mint and Garlic (Vg)

I love the peppery crunch of radishes but I know a lot of people don't. If you think you don't like radishes I would urge you to try this salad. Marinating them softens the flesh and they absorb the flavours of mint and garlic. It is served rather like an Indian Chutney, in small helpings with savoury dishes.

· *1 bunch of radishes*
· *1 clove of garlic*
· *1 bunch of mint*
· *15 ml olive oil*
· *15 ml white wine vinegar*
· *Salt and pepper to taste*

Slice the radishes very thinly, approximately 1 mm thick.

Peel and mince the garlic really finely. If you have a garlic crusher, use it: I know it wastes garlic but it does crush it finely.

Chop the mint finely.

Mix the olive oil and vinegar and season to taste.

In a shallow dish, mix the radishes with the mint, garlic and dressing. Put in the fridge and leave for at least 1 hour. You can leave it overnight.

Remove the salad from the fridge at least an hour before you want to eat it, it should be room temperature, not chilled. This salad is lovely with feta cheese and chard börek as a light lunch or a starter.

Coleslaw (Vg)

I love coleslaw in mid-winter when fresh salad leaves are a faint memory of summer. Keep it simple: crisp cabbage, freshly grated carrot, a good oil and vinegar dressing. That's it.

Serves 4

- *1 small head of cabbage*
- *2 medium carrots*
- *15 ml olive oil*
- *15 ml white wine vinegar*
- *Salt and pepper*

Cut the cabbage in half and remove the course inner ribs. Finely slice the cabbage and coarsely grate the carrots. Combine in a serving bowl. Mix the oil and vinegar and season to taste. Combine all the ingredients and serve. This is lovely with the Winter Squash Tart and some boiled potatoes dressed with olive oil and garlic.

Basmati Rice

Okay, it's not a vegetable but then nor are courgettes, tomatoes, peppers or aubergines. They are fruits as my pedantic partner Roy is forever pointing out.

However, it's an excellent side dish with many of these recipes. Rice is just rice right? Wrong. The way you cook rice makes a huge difference to the texture and the flavour. If you bung it in a pan and cover it with loads of water, boil it and then drain it, you lose all the goodness and flavour. Unsurprisingly, it was Madhur Jaffrey who taught me (not personally) to cook it properly. This is from *An Invitation to Indian Cooking*. Thank you Madhur.

Serves 4–6.

- 300 g basmati rice
- 450 ml water
- 20 g butter
- 2 tsp salt

First you need to soak your rice for half an hour. Put it in a bowl with the salt and cover well with water. After half an hour drain. Then leave it for 5–10 minutes (or longer).

In the pan in which you are going to cook the rice melt the butter over a low heat. Add the rice to the pan and stir well for about 2 minutes so that every grain is covered and the rice has started to absorb the butter. Add the water, cover the pan with a piece of aluminium foil and tuck it over the sides of the pan and then add the lid. Tightly. You want to make it as airtight as possible. It won't be completely.

Bring to the boil – you will know when it has because the foil will balloon upwards – then turn the heat to low and cook for approximately 15–20 minutes.

Once all the water has been absorbed turn the heat off and leave to settle. It will keep warm for up to 30 minutes.

Don't worry if you have slightly overcooked it. By leaving it to stand the rice will expel excess water and any dried grain will absorb it.

Rice With Nuts and Raisins (Vg)

This is based on a Madhur Jaffrey dish in *Eastern Vegetarian Cooking*. It's a great dish for a party, and this is precisely when I make it: for our annual late summer party.

- 600 g basmati rice
- 900 ml water
- 10 tbsp sunflower oil
- 20 g of blanched, slivered almonds
- 25 g raw shelled peanuts
- 25 g raw cashew nuts
- 20 g sesame seeds
- 60 g raisins
- 1 onion
- 4 cloves of garlic
- 2 cm piece of fresh ginger
- 1 fresh chilli
- 1 tsp cumin
- 1½ tsp salt

Put the rice in a bowl with 1½ tsp of salt and cover with water. Soak for half an hour, then drain and leave a rice in the strainer or sieve.

Turn the oven to 170˚C. Put the sesame seeds in a small heavy frying pan and roast over a low heat, shaking the pan regularly to ensure even cooking. Heat 1 tbsp of sunflower oil in a small heavy frying pan and cook the other nuts in batches, transferring to a plate with some kitchen towel. Add the raisins to the same pan. Once they puff up they are done.

Slice the onion finely. Peel and finely chop the garlic. Peel and finely grate the ginger. De-seed and finely chop the chilli.

In a large heavy ovenproof casserole (I use an old Le Creuset pot) heat about 4 tbsps of sunflower oil. Add the onion and cook over a low heat until soft. Add the garlic, ginger, chilli and cumin and cook for a couple of minutes, before adding the rice and salt. Stir well for a couple of minutes to ensure that all the rice grains are well coated in oil. Then add the water, turn up the heat and bring to the boil.

Reduce the heat and simmer, uncovered, until almost all the water has evaporated. There should be a little in the bottom of the pan. Turn off the heat and cover the pan with aluminium foil, crimping it around the top of the pan, then add the lid.

Cook in the centre of the oven for 20–25 minutes or until the rice is cooked through. Don't worry if you have overcooked it. Bring it out of the oven and leave it to stand, covered, for at least half an hour. By leaving it to stand the rice will expel excess water and any dried grain will absorb it.

Turn the rice onto a platter or large bowl and just before serving scatter on the nuts and raisins. This dish can be served hot or cold.

Chapter 6
Sugar

At the height of his literary powers Salman Rushdie wrote the immortal line "Naughty but nice." I think that pretty much describes this chapter. We all know that sugar is bad for you, but we all need a sweet treat from time to time. I've put cakes, biscuits and pudding all in one section and it is quite short because, frankly, I shouldn't be encouraging you to eat them.

I don't have a very sweet tooth, so I can be fairly virtuous at little personal cost – not so much when faced with a plate of chips drenched in malt vinegar and salt, straight from our local chippie. Anyway, back to the sugar. These recipes do contain some quite expensive ingredients so just keep them for special occasions or to drown out the existential angst of modern life.

~~~~~~~~~~~~~ *Sweet Pastry* ~~~~~~~~~~~~~

- 90 g corn flour (fine polenta)
- 50 g rice flour
- 30 g tapioca flour
- 20 g gram flour
- 30 g icing sugar
- ½ tsp xanthan gum
- 75 g butter or olive based margarine
- 1 egg

Sift the flours and icing sugar together in a bowl with the xanthan gum. Rub in the butter until you have the texture of fine breadcrumbs.

Beat the egg in a separate bowl, and add gradually to the mixture until it comes together in a ball. You may not need all the egg.

You can use straight away or store in the fridge overnight.

- 3 large ripe pears approx 500–600 g (or you can use poached pears see previous recipe)
- 130 g rice flour
- 30 g tapioca flour
- 15 g ground almonds
- 2 tsp baking powder
- 2 tsp ground ginger
- 1 tsp mixed spice
- 120 g demerara sugar
- 85 g butter or olive oil spread
- 2 eggs
- 50 ml milk
- 2–3 tbsp brandy
- 1–2 tbsp golden syrup

I specify 1–2 tbsp of golden syrup because, let's face it, the stuff is so viscous it's impossible to measure accurately. I put a tablespoon into the tin and fill it, but there is always a lot adhering to the outside of the spoon. It's not critical.

Line a deep, round 23 cm diameter spring-form cake tin with baking parchment. Preheat the oven to 180°C.

Beat the butter or olive oil spread and sugar together until light and fluffy. Beat the eggs and add them, then the rice and tapioca flours, ground almonds, ginger, mixed spice, and baking powder. Mix well.

Add the milk to the mixture along with the brandy and syrup. Make sure you have incorporated everything well.

Peel and core the pears and chop them into 1–1.5 cm cubes. Add the pears to the batter and mix well. Pour into your prepared tin.

Bake for 30 minutes until risen and golden. Test with a skewer, and if it's a bit underdone give it another 5 minutes. It's ready when the skewer comes out clean.

This is based on a recipe from *Moro*. The original uses quince paste, but not having any at the time I first made it, I used homemade crab-apple jelly. I have since made it using (a rather superior) shop bought raspberry jam a friend gave me, and my friend Joan's homemade lemon curd. All are delicious. Use whatever sweet spread you like – just use the best quality you can afford.

- *1 quantity of sweet pastry*

Filling

- *130 g crab-apple, bramble or other jelly*
- *230 g raw almonds*
- *Finely grated zest of 1 large lemon*
- *1 tsp ground cinnamon*
- *40 ml brandy*
- *115 g butter*
- *75 g soft brown or muscovado sugar*
- *2 eggs*

Preheat the oven to 180°C.

Using your hands push the pastry across the bottom of a 23 cm diameter flan dish and up the sides. You don't need to grease the dish as the pastry will come away from the sides cleanly. Tidy the top and keep a little for patching in case any cracks appear during the blind baking. Prick the base all over with a fork, and line with baking parchment and baking beans. Cook for 10 minutes.

Remove from oven, remove the beans and parchment and put into the oven for a further 5 minutes. Remove from oven and allow the pastry case to cool.

Meanwhile prepare the filling. You can blanch and skin the almonds if you wish. Personally I don't. Put them in a food processor and blitz them until they are the texture of cous cous. If you don't possess a food processor you could put them in a paper bag and bash them with a wooden rolling pin or process them in batches in a pestle and mortar. This is quite hard work so if you are using that method by all means substitute a softer nut like a walnut or pecan.

Mix the almonds with the lemon zest, cinnamon and brandy. Stir well and leave to blend for 5–10 minutes.

Cream the butter and sugar together and beat in the eggs, one at a time. Add the almonds and mix thoroughly.

Spoon the jelly into the pastry case and spread gently across the base. Spoon the almond mixture on top of the jelly and spread roughly across the tart, to the edges. Bake the dish in the centre of the oven for approximately 30 minutes until set. This is very good served with thick Greek-style yoghurt.

When I was a child and stayed with my grandparents in Doncaster, my grandmother would sometimes take me and my cousin Gail down to a bakery near the Winning Post bus stop and buy cheesecakes. They were individual tarts with a curd cheese filling with currants. That was what cheesecake meant to me, until the invasion in the 1980s of the American version with, for me, an overly rich and sweet confection atop a base of broken biscuits. I searched in vain for years amongst my many cookbooks for a recipe for what I remembered. Then recently I found some references to seventeenth-century cheesecake whilst noodling around on the internet, and found a series of recipes. Using inspiration from those recipes this is my attempt to recreate that memory.

I have used mascarpone, but you could use curd cheese. Make sure you take the eggs out of the fridge well before you want to make the tart. You only need the yolks in this recipe, but I recently discovered that you can freeze egg whites, so you don't need to immediately find a recipe requiring just egg whites.

- *1 quantity of sweet pastry*

For the filling:

- *250 g mascarpone*
- *2 eggs, separated*
- *30 g sugar*
- *45 ml rosewater*

- *50 g currants*
- *1 tbsp lemon juice*
- *1 tsp cinnamon*
- *¼ tsp grated nutmeg*

Preheat the oven to 180°C.

Using your hands push the pastry across the bottom of a 23 cm diameter flan dish and up the sides. You don't need to grease the dish as the pastry will come away from the sides cleanly. Tidy the top and keep a little for patching in case any cracks appear during the blind baking. Prick the base all over with a fork, and line with baking parchment and baking beans. Cook for 10 minutes.

Remove from oven, remove the beans and parchment and put into the oven for a further 5–10 minutes to crisp the base.

Whilst the shell is baking, make the filling.

Put the mascarpone and egg yolks in a bowl and beat together well. If you had some egg left over from making the pastry add it to the bowl. Add the sugar, currants, lemon juice, rose water and spices and combine well. Pour the mixture into the pastry case and place the tart in the oven immediately.

Cook for 15 minutes by which time the top should be golden. Turn the oven down to 150°C and bake for a further 5–10 minutes. Remove from the oven and leave it to cool.

- *12 pears, whichever variety you like*
- *2 cinnamon sticks and 3 star anise OR 4 cloves and 4 green cardamom pods*
- *3 sprigs of sweet cicely (if you have it, it is not essential)*
- *30 g sugar (40-45 g if you are not using sweet cicely)*
- *Water to cover*

Sweet cicely is a native herb and useful for planting in shady parts of the garden. The leaves added to any fruit you are cooking will reduce the amount of sugar you need to add.

Peel the pears, cut in half and each half in three lengthwise, and core. Put the pear pieces in a large saucepan or casserole, add the cinnamon, sweet cicely (if you are using it) and star anise, and sprinkle the sugar over. Put enough water in to barely cover the pears.

Put on a high heat until the water is coming to a simmer, then turn down to the lowest heat. Keep a careful eye on the pan and let it just simmer for 10 minutes.

Using a slotted spoon remove the pears and put on a plate to cool. Remove the sweet cicely.

Turn the heat up to full and boil the liquid until very reduced. It will become a lovely warm brown colour. Turn off the heat and let it cool with the spices. It will be slightly sweet and infused with the taste of cinnamon and star anise. You can serve the pears with a little of the syrup with some thick Greek yoghurt or pouring cream.

You can also freeze them in tubs with a little of the syrup in each tub. And you can use them to make Pear and Ginger Cake.

Hazelnut and Cranberry Dark Chocolates (Vg)

Having made the white chocolate and almond confections *(see on page 148)* I decided to experiment with other chocolate and nut combinations. Dark chocolate is much easier to work with than white. Always start with the most complicated, that's me all over.

- *100 g good quality free trade dark chocolate*
- *15 g hazelnuts*
- *15 g dried cranberries*
- *6 mini muffin cases*

Roast the hazelnuts for approximately 10 minutes in a preheated oven at 180°C. Allow to cool. You can do this at any time when you have the oven on for something else, then store them in a jar or other air tight container.

Break the chocolate into small even pieces and place in a bowl. Boil some water in a kettle, pour it into a small saucepan to a depth of no more than 5 cm and set on a very low heat. The bowl should sit snugly on the top of the saucepan but, importantly, should not touch the water. Once it starts to melt, stir the chocolate with a dry spoon. Do not allow any liquid to touch the chocolate.

Set out six mini muffin cases in a flat bottomed dish that can go in the fridge.

Once the chocolate has melted take it off the heat and add the hazelnuts and dried cranberries and mix together thoroughly. Let it stand for a couple of minutes to cool slightly.

Using a teaspoon divide the mixture evenly between the mini muffin cases. Take your time. The chocolate will remain liquid for quite some time and it is easier to work with once it has cooled a little.

Let them stand for half an hour, then put them in the fridge to firm up.

Alessia runs the B&B Città dei Templi in Agrigento, Sicily. She is a warm hostess who offers spacious, comfortable rooms and an amazing breakfast. You're a coeliac? No problem. Her cousin runs a shop specializing in gluten free products. She will ply you with gluten free cannoli, pizza, very good bread and cakes. And *very* good coffee.

On our second morning, having established I liked a more savoury breakfast, I had stuffed myself with some pizza and half a large roll with some salami. I asked her if it would be okay to take the rest of the roll for later. Yes, yes, and take some salami with it. And you must have this she said proffering a small sweetmeat. It's almond she confided, wrapping it up in a napkin for me, before dashing to her father's bakery next door to get an ordinary almond biscuit for my partner Roy so he didn't feel left out.

We had returned to Palermo by the time I ate my leftovers. What a revelation! I don't have the recipe but it seemed to me that it was just – just! – roasted almonds in white chocolate. It took me a while to get the method right, but the flavour was there right away. Check the chocolate packaging carefully: some brands may contain traces of gluten.

If you cannot get hold of mini muffin cases I would down-size to sweet cases; up-scaling to muffin cases would be excessive.

- 100 g good quality fair trade white chocolate
- 20 g whole almonds
- 6 mini muffin cases

Roast the almonds for approximately 10 minutes in a preheated oven at 180°C. Allow to cool. You can do this at any time when you have the oven on for something else, then store them in a jar or other air tight container.

Break the chocolate into small even pieces and place in a bowl. Boil some water in a kettle, pour it into a small saucepan to a depth of no more than 5 cm and set on a very low heat. The bowl should sit snugly on the top of the saucepan but, importantly, should not touch the water. Once it starts to melt, stir the chocolate with a dry spoon. Do not allow any liquid to touch the chocolate.

Set out six mini muffin cases in a flat bottomed dish that can go in the fridge. White chocolate does not become as liquid as milk or plain chocolate so it is not as easy to pour. Once it is soft, keeping the bowl over the pan of water, on the heat, add the almonds and mix together thoroughly.

Use two teaspoons to divide the mixture between the six cases. Leave to stand for 15 minutes so that the chocolate can settle into the cases. Place in the fridge for an hour. Store in an airtight container in a cool larder or similar, before devouring. Alternatively, they make nice presents.

Walnut and Raisin Dark Chocolates (Vg)

This Is another good combination. Use the method above.

- 100 g good quality free trade dark chocolate
- 15 g walnuts
- 15 g raisins
- 6 mini muffin cases

This is a good way to help use up a glut of courgettes.

- *3 medium courgettes about 350 g*
- *200 g fine polenta*
- *100 g ground almonds*
- *200 g soft brown sugar*
- *3 eggs*
- *125 g sunflower oil*
- *2 tsp baking powder*
- *1 tsp bicarbonate of soda*
- *2 tsp ground cardamom*
- *Zest of 2 lemons*
- *Juice of 1 lemon*

Set your oven to 180°C. Line a 23 cm diameter round, spring-form tin with baking parchment.

Top and tail the courgettes and grate them. You don't need to peel them.

In a large bowl beat the eggs with the sugar and oil.

Sift in the polenta and ground almonds with the cardamom, baking powder and bicarbonate of soda. Add the lemon zest and juice and the courgettes and mix well together. The mixture will be the consistency of a batter. Don't worry if it looks runny, it's meant to.

Pour the mixture into your prepared cake tin and put into the oven. It will take 45–50 minutes.

Test with a skewer: if it comes out clean it's done. Test in a number of places. The first time I made this although the skewer came out clean, it was not cooked in the middle, and as it cooled it sank. I had to re-cook it. It looked a complete mess, like the aftermath of a volcanic eruption, but it tasted fine, even if the texture was a little dense, not unlike the cook. It's by making mistakes that we learn. Very few of our mistakes are inedible. We just know to do it differently next time.

The original recipe this is based on is from Delia Smith's *Book of Cakes*. It is so simple a child of five could make it, but it tastes as though it is a lot more complicated to make. It has been my go-to recipe whenever I am asked to make a cake for a cake sale. It's very quick **except** that you do need to organise yourself the night before. Soak the raisins in the cold tea overnight. You can use any tea, but the better the tea, the better the taste of the finished loaf.

- *225 g raisins*
- *175 g demerara sugar*
- *100 g fine polenta*
- *75 g tapioca flour*
- *50 g brown rice flour*
- *170 ml cold Darjeeling tea*

- *2 tsp xanthan gum*
- *1 tsp baking powder*
- *1 tsp ground cinnamon*
- *1 tbsp glycerin*
- *1 egg, beaten*

Make a small pot or mug of tea and leave to cool. Put the raisins in a small bowl and pour 170 ml of tea over them and leave overnight.

Preheat the oven to 180°C. Line a 2 lb loaf tin with greaseproof paper.

Tip your soaked raisins into a mixing bowl and fold in all the dry ingredients. Add the glycerin and egg and combine well. Spoon the mixture into the prepared tin and place in the centre of the oven. Bake for approximately 50 minutes. Check regularly and if the top is browning too quickly turn the temperature down to 150°C–160°C.

When the loaf is cooked (you can test this by putting a skewer into the loaf; if it comes out clean the loaf is cooked) remove from the oven and leave it to stand in its tin for 10–15 minutes. Then turn out onto a wire tray and remove the paper. Leave the loaf to cool and then store in an airtight container. This loaf can be eaten as it is, served with yoghurt as a pudding or spread with butter.

These biscuits are sharp with lemon, hard outside and soft within. They are delicious with a cup of tea or coffee, or as a simple end to a meal with friends, served with a good dessert wine.

Makes about 30

- *200 g ground almonds*
- *200 g rice flour*
- *200 g demerara sugar*
- *Grated zest and juice of 1 lemon*
- *2 egg whites*
- *Pinch of cream of tartar, or a few drops of lemon juice or white wine vinegar*

Preheat the oven to 160°C and line a large baking sheet with baking parchment.

Mix the ground almonds and rice flour in a large bowl with 100 g of the sugar and the lemon zest.

Beat the egg whites with the cream of tartar, until they are foamy white, then add the remaining sugar and beat until the mixture is glossy. You do not need it to be stiff as when making meringues.

Add the egg and lemon juice to the almond mixture and gently stir, you may need to use your hands at this point to incorporate all the ingredients. The mixture will still be quite crumbly but will stay together when you mould it with your hands.

Shape the mixture into ovals about the size of a fat Medjool date and place on the baking tray. You can put them quite close together as the mixture does not spread. Bake for 15–20 minutes, checking regularly, until they are golden brown. Transfer to a wire rack to cool before storing in an airtight container.

I call these Gems because they remind me of the Little Gems we used to have at birthday party teas when I was a child. No? Oh well, you're probably a lot younger than me. They had a crisp biscuit base and a hard sugar topping, like a Mr Whippy ice-cream, in a range of pastel colours. Shockingly bad for you I'm sure. These aren't a lot better for you but you aren't going to eat them often are you?

- 90 g brown rice flour
- 30 g tapioca flour
- 20 g gram flour
- 45 g soft brown sugar
- 45 g butter or olive oil spread
- ½ tsp of baking powder
- ½ tsp xanthan gum
- ½ tsp ground cardamom
- Finely grated zest ½–1 lemon
- 1 egg

Preheat the oven to 150°C. Line two baking sheets with baking parchment.

In a bowl, with a fork, mix together the butter and sugar. Add the egg and beat well. Sift the flours and all dry goods into the mix, and add the lemon zest. Mix thoroughly.

Take cherry-sized pieces and place on baking sheet. Dipping a fork in icing sugar or rice flour, use it to slightly flatten the biscuits. Put the trays in the oven and bake at 150°C for 20 minutes. Turn down to 100°C and cook for a further 20 minutes.

When the bases of the biscuits no longer feel soft they are ready. Leave to cool in the trays then transfer them to a wire cooling rack. Store in an airtight container. Nice with a cup of tea or a glass of sherry, just one, oh okay, make it two.

Of course they aren't really shortbread but because they are made with the sweet shortcrust pastry as the base of the recipe, they are a nice short biscuit. They were inspired by a Jeremy Lee recipe I read recently in the *Guardian*. They are not very sweet, which I like. They would be nice served with ice-cream. If you prefer your biscuits sweeter, substitute 20 g of polenta for another 20 g of icing sugar.

- *1 quantity of sweet shortcrust pastry **minus** the egg*
- *1 egg*
- *Zest of 1 orange*
- *1 tsp fennel seeds*
- *Additional brown rice flour*

Sift the flours in the usual way with the xanthan gum and rub in the olive oil spread. Add the orange zest and fennel seeds and mix thoroughly. Add the egg and mix until the dough comes together. Divide the dough in 2.

Cut 2 pieces of baking parchment, approximately 20–30 cm. Sprinkle with brown rice flour. Put each piece of dough on a sheet of baking parchment and form into a thick sausage of 3–4 cm diameter. Flatten the ends. Wrap the parchment around the dough and twist the ends so that you end up with something like a Christmas cracker. Chill in the fridge overnight.

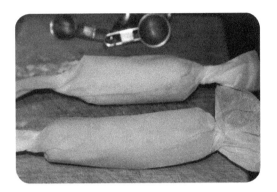

Preheat the oven to 180°C. Line 2 large baking sheets with baking parchment.

Take the first lot of dough out of the fridge and open the baking parchment. Leave the dough on the parchment. Take a sharp knife and slice the dough into rounds approximately 3 mm thick. As you cut them you will find they flatten slightly so you do not get a perfect disc. But I rather like this: they look a bit like fat orange segments which is appropriate don't you think? Repeat with the second lot of dough.

Bake in the oven for 10 minutes by which time they will have turned golden. Turn the oven down to 150°C and bake for a further 5 minutes. Remove from the oven and leave to cool. Store in an airtight container.

First make your rhubarb gin *(see page 196)*. The fruit left over from making fruit-flavoured alcohols can be used to make ice-cream. Well, it would be a shame to waste it, wouldn't it?

You don't have to have an ice-cream maker to make ice-cream, but it does make it easier. You can buy a very basic one quite cheaply: mine cost less than £30. Alternatively you can put the ice-cream in a shallow covered tub in the freezer, and regularly take it out and vigorously re-mix to prevent ice crystals forming. It's a bit of a faff, but home-made ice-cream is so much better than shop bought.

For the rhubarb:

- 200 g leftover rhubarb from your gin bottle (doesn't that sound wonderfully decadent?)
- Juice of 1 large orange
- 15 g sugar

For the custard:

- 300 ml full cream milk
- 300 ml double cream
- 3 large egg yolks
- 80 g sugar

Rhubarb which has been preserved in alcohol is quite turgid and does not cook down like fresh rhubarb, so you need to cook it with orange juice rather than water.

Put the rhubarb in a saucepan with the sugar and orange juice. Cover and bring it to the boil and then cook on a low heat for approximately 15 minutes. Remove the lid and leave to cool.

Pour the milk into a heavy bottomed pan and heat until just shy of boiling. Leave to cool.

Beat the eggs with the sugar. Add the cooled milk and then put on a low heat and stir constantly until the mixture thickens. Pour into a clean bowl and leave to cool. If it looks as if it has curdled slightly whisk vigorously for several minutes. Once cool, whisk in the cream then cover and refrigerate until completely chilled.

Whisk the fruit into the chilled custard, then freeze according to the instructions on your ice-cream maker or put in the freezer and regularly re-mix.

This is a good recipe for a glut or if your local market stall is selling off fruit at the end of the day. In 2016 we had an amazing strawberry crop, too much to use at the time, so to stop the fruit spoiling I puréed a load and froze it.

Two years later I found them again and decided to make ice-cream. You can use a smaller quantity of strawberries, but obviously the more you use the stronger the strawberry flavour will be.

- *Approximately 450 g fresh or frozen strawberries.*

For the custard:

- *300 ml full cream milk*
- *300 ml double cream*
- *3 large egg yolks*
- *80 g sugar*

First make the custard.

Pour the milk into a heavy bottomed pan and heat until just shy of boiling. Leave to cool.

Beat the eggs with the sugar. Add the cooled milk and then put on a low heat and stir constantly until the mixture thickens. Pour into a clean bowl and leave to cool. If it looks as if it has curdled slightly whisk vigorously for several minutes. Once cool, whisk in the cream then cover and refrigerate until completely chilled. You can leave it overnight.

Remove the strawberry leaves and hull them. Put them into a food processor and whizz them until you have a thick purée.

Remove the chilled custard from the fridge and stir in the strawberry purée, combining thoroughly.

Freeze according to the instructions on your ice-cream maker or put in the freezer and regularly re-mix.

Chapter 7

Sauces, Preserves and Drinks

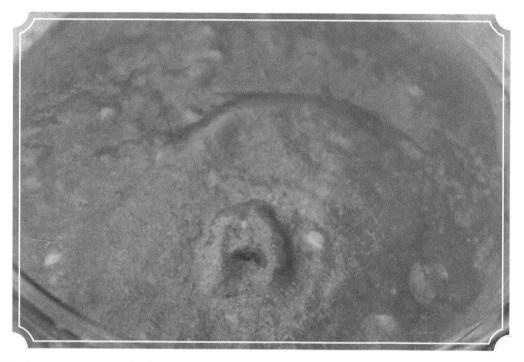

This is a sauce to make in early autumn when you have a glut of tomatoes. If you don't grow your own, get the best locally grown tomatoes you can. Don't be tempted to use imported supermarket tomatoes, they taste of nothing and your passata will similarly taste of nothing. You can use any size, variety or colour, and any mixture of tomatoes you like. Just make sure they're tasty. This is based on Rachel Roddy's recipe for tomato sauce in *Five Quarters*. I omit the salt as I sometimes use passata in recipes with legumes, and cooking them with salt will make them tough. You can season in your final recipe. I freeze my passata: it makes a wonderful treat, as taste of summer, in the depths of winter. I would encourage you to invest in a food mill, but you could use a coarse sieve instead.

- *1 kg tomatoes*
- *1–2 cloves of garlic, depending on size*
- *Two sprigs of basil*

Cut your tomatoes in halves or quarters depending on size, and put in a saucepan. Cook, covered, on a medium heat for a few minutes then bash the tomatoes with a wooden spoon to encourage the juice to flow, and cook for another 5–10 minutes until they start to collapse. Place the food mill, or sieve, over a deep bowl. Using the coarsest disc on your food mill process the tomatoes in batches until all that is left in the mill is skin. If you are using a sieve use a wooden spoon to mash the tomatoes through into the bowl.

Peel and, using the heel of your hand and the flat blade of a kitchen knife, crush the garlic so it is still whole, but broken. Transfer the tomato pulp back into the saucepan, and add the garlic and basil. Set over a medium heat and leave to bubble away for 20–30 minutes, checking regularly. You want a thick sauce.

Bechamel Sauce

- 25 g butter
- 25 g gram flour
- 350–400 ml whole milk
- Salt and pepper

You can make a perfectly acceptable béchamel sauce using gram or cornflour instead of wheat flour. Use an olive oil based spread and soy milk to make this sauce suitable for vegans.

Melt the butter in a small saucepan. Sift in the gram flour to avoid getting lumps. Combine thoroughly and cook for a couple of minutes, stirring continuously. Gradually add the milk making sure that you incorporate it thoroughly into the sauce before adding more. Use more milk if you want a thinner sauce. Season to taste.

The quantities of fruit in this recipe are arbitrary. We were going on holiday and I had a number of citrus fruits in a bowl and didn't want to waste them so popped them in the freezer. You can use any combination of citrus for this marmalade or just oranges, it's up to you. If you buy Seville oranges in the winter to make marmalade and run out of time, do the same thing. Keep them frozen until you have the time.

- *4 blood oranges if you can find them, or any other orange*
- *2 lemons*
- *5 limes*
- *1.2 litres water*
- *Approx 900 g sugar*

Cut all the fruits in half and squeeze out the juice. Reserve the pips. Store the juice in a jug in the fridge.

Put the pips and pith in a piece of muslin and secure with string.

Place the shells of the fruit in a preserving pan or large saucepan with the water and the muslin bag. Bring to the boil, turn down the heat, half cover and simmer for 1 hour.

Allow the contents of the pan to cool then drain the contents into a large bowl through a colander.

Scoop the flesh out of the fruit shells and return to the pan along with the liquor, sugar and fruit juice.

Slice as much of the peel as you want to use as thickly or thinly as you like, or into small pieces. For this recipe I used the peel of 3 oranges and 1 of the lemons. Add to the pan.

Sterilise a number of jam jars by putting them, without their lids, in the oven on a low heat for 30 minutes. Turn off the oven.

Heat the pan gently, stirring all the time, until the sugar has dissolved.

Bring to the boil and boil vigorously for about 20 minutes. Test for a set by putting a small amount on a saucer and putting in the fridge for 2 minutes. If it forms a skin and wrinkles when pushed with a finger it's done.

Carefully remove the jars from the oven using oven gloves. Ladle the marmalade into the jars and put the lids on. This process is much easier if you have a jam funnel. Once cool make sure the lids are screwed on tightly and label the jars.

Incidentally, apropos of nothing in particular, I have two lemon squeezers, one plastic and one glass. I have found the glass one to be much better at extracting maximum juice. Just a thought.

Seville Orange Marmalade (Vg)

On the day Storm Georgina crossed Britain I decided to make this marmalade. Sheltering from high winds and driving rain in a warm kitchen suffused with the scent of citrus seemed the best option. You will need a jelly bag and some apparatus from which to hang it. My partner Roy constructed a small wooden gallows for me many years ago which I use to this day.

- 8 Seville oranges
- 1 lemon
- 2.5 litres of water
- Sugar

Start by removing the zest of the fruit. You can pare the zest with a sharp knife and then slice it thinly, but to be honest that is a monumental faff and risks a slipped knife and cuts to the fingers. I find the quickest and easiest method is to use a lemon zester. Put the zest in a small pan with 300 ml of the water, bring to the boil and then simmer for 30 minutes. Leave to cool.

Cut the fruit into chunks and put in a preserving pan, pith, seeds, the lot. Put the rest of the water into the pan and bring to the boil. Simmer for an hour. The liquid should have reduced by approximately one-third. Leave to cool.

Sterilise your jelly bag by putting it in a small bowl and pouring boiling water over it. Pour away the water and set your jelly bag over a bowl on your chosen apparatus.

Strain the water from the zest into the pan with the fruit. Set the zest aside. Ladle the fruit and liquid into the jelly bag and leave to drain overnight.

The next day, discard the fruit and measure the resulting liquid. You will require 450 g of sugar per 600 ml of liquid.

Sterilise a number of jam jars by putting them, without their lids, in the oven on a low heat for 30 minutes. Turn off the oven.

Pour the liquid into a clean preserving pan over a gentle heat. Add the sugar, stirring constantly until it has dissolved. Many books on making preserves stress the importance of heating the sugar first. I never have and no one has ever complained. Add the reserved zest, bring to the boil and boil vigorously for 15–20 minutes or until the setting point has been reached. Test for a set by putting a small amount on a saucer and putting in the fridge for 2 minutes. If it forms a skin and wrinkles when pushed with a finger it's done.

Carefully remove the jars from the oven using oven gloves. Ladle the marmalade into the jars, using a jam funnel if you have one, and put the lids on. Once cool make sure the lids are screwed on tightly and label the jars.

Crab-Apple Jelly (Vg)

We have three crab-apple trees in the garden. One is quite old and doesn't fruit well and what fruit it produces is gnarled and scabbed. But the blossom is gorgeous in the late spring and it is home to a wild dog rose, so despite an odd woolly growth on the trunk we keep it. Two or three years ago we planted two more: Jelly King and John Downie, which is an eater. They have produced a little, but not much, fruit so far. I can be patient. But in a corner of the allotment site, there is a piece of land managed (I use the term loosely) by the Council and called a Nature Reserve. It is completely overgrown, but close to the fence is a crab-apple tree which produce the most beautiful fruit and these we harvest.

- 2 kg crab-apples
- 1.5 litres water
- 2 lemons
- 5 green cardamoms
- Sugar

Thoroughly wash the fruit to remove any dust etc. then roughly chop it and put in a preserving pan along with all their seeds, stalks etc. Pour over the water and bring to the boil. Simmer for 1–1 ½ hours. Leave to cool.

Strain the contents through a jelly bag overnight. You need some kind of device for suspending the bag over a bowl. My partner Roy constructed one for me years ago out of bits of old shelves and some doweling. It means that the size of bowl I can use is restricted, so I have to drain through as much liquid as I can, then perform a conjuring trick to replace the bowl with another, and so on.

Do not be tempted to squeeze the bag to get more juice out: it will make the resulting jelly cloudy.

Sterilise a number of jam jars by putting them, without their lids, in the oven on a low heat for 30 minutes. Turn off the oven.

You need to measure the volume of juice you have. Pour it into the cleaned preserving pan. Add 450 g of sugar to each 600 ml of liquid, then bring gradually to the boil, stirring all the while, until the sugar has completely dissolved.

Squeeze the two lemons and add the juice to the pan. Slice up the peel and place in a small muslin bag along with the cardamom pods, and tie it with string. I tend to use bits of old cotton from worn out pillow cases. Add to the pan.

Bring to the boil and boil vigorously for about 20 minutes. Test for a set by putting a small amount on a saucer and putting in the fridge for 2 minutes. If it forms a skin and wrinkles when pushed with a finger it's done.

Carefully remove the jars from the oven using oven gloves. Ladle the jelly into the jars, using a jam funnel if you have one, and put the lids on. Once cool make sure the lids are screwed on tightly and label the jars.

Japanese Quince Jelly (Vg)

Chaenomeles is a shrub often grown against a wall, with pretty small saucer shaped flowers in late spring. It produces fruit in the autumn which look like small quince, about the size of a large walnut, hence their popular name, Japanese Quince. Though grown as an ornamental, the fruit is edible and makes a very pleasant jelly. Adjust the amounts for however much fruit you can get hold of from your own garden or from a friend's. You can't buy them commercially.

- 1 kg Japanese Quince
- 3–3.5 litres water
- 1 lemon
- Sugar

Wash the fruit thoroughly to remove any dust etc, then chop the fruit roughly and place in a preserving pan together with the pips and stalks. Cover with the water, bring to the boil and simmer for 1–1½ hours. Allow to cool.

Strain the contents through a jelly bag over night. You need some kind of device for suspending the bag over a bowl. My partner Roy constructed one for me years ago out of bits of old shelves and some doweling. It means that the size of bowl I can use is restricted, so I have to drain through as much liquid as I can, then perform a conjuring trick to replace the bowl with another, and so on.

Do not be tempted to squeeze the bag to get more juice out: it will make the resulting jelly cloudy.

Sterilise a number of jam jars by putting them, without their lids, in the oven on a low heat for 30 minutes. Turn off the oven.

You need to measure the volume of juice you have. Pour it into the cleaned preserving pan. Add 450 g of sugar to each 600 ml of liquid, then bring gradually to the boil, stirring all the while, until the sugar has completely dissolved.

Squeeze the lemon and add the juice to the pan. Slice up the peel and place in a small muslin bag, and tie it with string. I tend to use bits of old cotton from worn out pillowcases. Add to the pan.

Bring to the boil and boil vigorously for about 20 minutes. Test for a set by putting a small amount on a saucer and putting in the fridge for 2 minutes. If it forms a skin and wrinkles when pushed with a finger it's done.

Carefully remove the jars from the oven using oven gloves. Ladle the jelly into the jars, using a jam funnel if you have one and put the lids on. Once cool make sure the lids are screwed on tightly and label the jars.

Autumn is the time to make chutneys as the apples and pears ripen. The original recipe for this chutney came from Elizabeth Ortiz's book of preserves *Clearly Delicious*. It has a gentle mellow flavour that marries well with milder cheese to have on crackers, or to serve alongside almond and potato croquettes with simple boiled potatoes and a salad.

- 1.5 kg pears
- 700 g onions
- 500 g tomatoes
- 2 green peppers
- 50 g raisins
- 900 ml white wine vinegar
- 450 g demerara sugar
- 15 g salt
- 1 tsp cinnamon
- ½ tsp ground cloves
- Pinch of cayenne pepper

Peel and core the pears, cut them into rough dice and put them in a preserving pan or large saucepan. Peel and slice the onions and add them to the pan.

Cut the peppers in two, discard all the seeds and any pith. Dice them into rough 1 cm squares.

Cover the tomatoes with boiling water and leave for 2 minutes. Drain and cover with cold water to stop them cooking further. Peel and chop and add to the pan.

Place the pan on the hob, bring to the boil and then turn the heat to low. Simmer for approximately 30 minutes until all the fruit and vegetables are soft.

Sterilise a number of jam jars by putting them, without their lids, in the oven on a low heat for 30 minutes. Turn off the oven.

Add all the other ingredients, stirring all the while, until the sugar has dissolved. Simmer the chutney over a low heat for 1–1½ hours until it has thickened and become unctuous and jammy.

Carefully remove the jars from the oven using oven gloves. Ladle the chutney into the jars, using a jam funnel if you have one, and put the lids on. Once cool make sure the lids are screwed on tightly and label the jars.

You can use any winter squash for this chutney.

- 1 kg winter squash flesh
- 1 kg apples
- 2 onions
- 450 ml white wine vinegar
- 300 g demerara sugar
- 2.5 cm cube of fresh ginger
- 2 fresh chillies, approximately 3 cm long
- 1 tsp ground cumin
- 1 tsp coriander seeds
- 1 tsp fennel seeds
- 1 tsp mustard seeks
- ½ tsp fenugreek seeds
- 2 tsp salt

Cut the squash in half and remove the seeds and the stringy fresh around them. Cut into wedges and peel, then grate the squash. Put the grated squash into a preserving pan or large saucepan.

Peel and core the apples and cut into rough 1 cm dice. Finely chop the onions. Add the apples and onions to the pan.

Deseed and finely chop the chillies, grate the ginger and add them to the pan.

Pour over the white wine vinegar and add the dry spices and stir well. Bring to the boil and then turn down the heat and simmer for 30 minutes.

Sterilise a number of jam jars by putting them, without their lids, in the oven on a low heat for 30 minutes. Turn off the oven.

Add the sugar and 1 tsp of the salt and mix well. Let it simmer for 1–1 ½ hours until all the liquid has been absorbed, stirring occasionally. Taste and add more salt if you wish.

Carefully remove the jars from the oven using oven gloves. Ladle the chutney into the jars, using a jam funnel if you have one, and put the lids on. Once cool make sure the lids are screwed on tightly and label the jars.

Leave for a couple of months to mature. It makes a nice relish with a simple dal and rice meal, or a spicy accompaniment to crackers and a good strong cheese such as Lincolnshire Poacher.

- 2 kg cherry plums
- 1 kg sugar
- 700 ml red wine vinegar
- 25 g root ginger, peeled weight
- 12 cloves
- 30 coriander seeds
- 10 allspice berries

This recipe is based on two which Jeremy Lee wrote in the *Guardian's* cookery column many years ago, one for Spiced Plums and one for Pickled Damsons. I still have the cutting. I don't have access to damsons, and where do you see them for sale these days? But I do have access to cherry plums. Our garden abuts an area of scrub and woodland where wild cherry plum trees grow alongside ash and elder and the occasional spindle. We pick the fruit of both the cherry plums and the elder, though not necessarily every year. There is only so much elderberry jelly you can eat or give away.

You could make this recipe with any small stone fruit. I have used plums and apricots, and cherries would also work well. You can pick up fruit in local markets quite cheaply at the end of the day when they are selling it off before it spoils.

Jeremy Lee starts his recipe "Prick the fruit all over with a silver fork. Nice touch." I do like his style. I don't possess a silver fork, but if you do by all means use it.

So, prick the fruit all over and put in a preserving pan or large saucepan.

Put the remaining ingredients in a separate pan and bring to the boil then reduce the heat and simmer for five minutes.

Pour the syrup over the fruit and leave it to cool. Once cool, cover the pan with a tea towel and leave it to sit overnight.

Sterilise a number of jam jars by putting them, without their lids, in the oven on a low heat for 30 minutes. Turn off the oven. Carefully remove the jars from the oven using oven gloves.

Strain the liquid from the pan and divide the cherry plums between the jars. Bring the pickling liquid to the boil and reduce it by one-third. Pour over fruits and seal the jars.

Spiced Blackberry Vinegar (Vg)

My grandmother and my Auntie Dorothy, both good Yorkshire women, used to make raspberry and blackberry vinegar in late summer to serve with Yorkshire pudding. This was proper Yorkshire pudding, not made in little pattie tins. The batter was poured into a large roasting tin, greased with dripping, and put into a hot oven, producing a billowy blanket, crisp without, soft within. It was cut into slabs and served with the vinegar before the main meal. Food designed to fill you up so you didn't need so much of the expensive meat and vegetables.

My version is not so sweet, designed more to use on salads or to add piquancy to a sauce.

- 800 g blackberries
- 280 ml red wine vinegar
- Demerara sugar

- 5–10 g cinnamon sticks
- 5–10 g cloves
- 5–10 g allspice berries

Crush the blackberries with the back of the wooden spoon and put in a large jar with the vinegar, and cover. Leave in a dark place for a week. Agitate the jar at least once each day.

Drain the contents of the jar through a jelly bag (I leave it overnight to try to get every last drop). Measure the resulting liquid and pour into a preserving pan or large saucepan.

Sterilise a number of bottles by putting them, without their lids or corks if you are using them, in the oven on a low heat for 30 minutes. Turn off the oven.

Tie the spices into a piece of muslin or cotton and secure with string.

For every 600 ml of liquid add 125 g of sugar. Add the bag of spices. Bring the liquid gradually to the boil stirring until the sugar has completely dissolved. Boil rapidly for 10 minutes.

Carefully remove the bottles from the oven using oven gloves. Using a funnel, ladle the vinegar into the bottles and put the lids on. Once cool make sure the lids are screwed on tightly or the corks are fully depressed, and label the bottles.

This is a classic ketchup to have with oily fish (just in case you eat fish), but it also goes really well with Lime and Ginger Lentil Cakes or with cheese and biscuits.

- 1 kg gooseberries
- 3 cloves garlic
- 1 tbsp salt
- 1 tsp cayenne pepper
- 1 tbsp mustard seeds
- 450 ml white wine vinegar
- 350 g demerara sugar

Chop the gooseberries and place in a preserving pan or large saucepan.

Peel and finely chop the garlic and add to the pan. Put in all the remaining ingredients.

Sterilise a number of bottles by putting them, without their lids or corks if you are using them, in the oven on a low heat for 30 minutes. Turn off the oven.

Bring the pan to the boil, stirring until the sugar has completely dissolved. Cover and simmer for 30 minutes until the gooseberries are really soft and collapsed.

Strain through a fine sieve into a large jug (it makes it easier to bottle), pressing down the fruit to extract all the liquid.

Carefully remove the bottles from the oven using oven gloves. Using a funnel, pour the ketchup into the bottles and put the lids on. Once cool make sure the lids are screwed on tightly or the corks are fully depressed, and label the bottles.

If you grow sweet cicely, or know someone who does, make this in the early summer when the plant first goes to seed and then store it for a comforting drink in the dark days of winter. Gather the seeds when they are plump and green before they turn black. The resulting drink has a pleasantly aniseed flavour. You don't need to add the other botanicals but it does give a greater depth of flavour.

- *1 bottle of vodka*
- *A small handful of sweet cicely seeds, approximately 20 g*
- *2 sprigs of thyme*
- *2 bay leaves*
- *½ tsp coriander seeds*

You don't need expensive vodka to do this. Use a cheap supermarket own-brand.

Sterilise a large jar or demijohn and allow it to cool.

Wash the sweet cicely seeds and herbs and allow to dry.

Place the sweet cicely and coriander seeds in the jar along with the herbs. Pour over the vodka and store in a dark place for a week, in the larder if you have one. If you don't the cupboard under the stairs or any other dark cupboard will do nicely. Strain the vodka through a fine sieve and bottle.

- *350 ml sweet cicely vodka*
- *50 g demerara sugar*

First make your sweet cicely vodka, see previous page.

Sterilise a bottle that will hold up to 400 ml. Decant 350 ml of your vodka into it and add 50 g of demerara sugar.

Store the bottle in a dark place, in the larder if you have one. If you don't the cupboard under the stairs or any other dark cupboard will do nicely. You can shake the jar every couple of days, but it's not essential. After a week all the sugar will have dissolved and your liqueur is ready. Enjoy.

Rhubarb Gin (Vg)

The rhubarb turns the gin a beautiful pink and imparts a faint taste of grapefruit. It makes a lovely gin and tonic.

You don't need expensive gin to do this. Use a cheap supermarket own-brand.

- *A 70 cl bottle of gin*
- *400 g rhubarb*
- *50 g demerara sugar*
- *Juice of ½ a lemon*

Sterilise a large jar or demijohn in the oven and allow it to cool.

Chop the rhubarb into rough chunks and put them in the jar.

Sprinkle over the sugar and the lemon juice, and pour over the gin. Secure the lid or cork the jar.

Store the jar in a dark place, in the larder if you have one. If you don't the cupboard under the stairs or any other dark cupboard will do nicely. You can shake the jar every couple of days, but it's not essential. Leave for at least 3 weeks or up to 6: all the sugar will have dissolved and your gin is ready. Decant and enjoy.

You can use the rhubarb to make puddings. However, the gin will have stiffened the stems so they won't cook down in the same way. Use a little orange juice instead of water (see the Rhubarb Gin Ice-cream recipe *on page 158*).

Crème de Mûre (Vg)

- 600 g blackberries, fresh or frozen
- 750 ml bottle of good quality red wine
- 500 g sugar
- 1 large glass of gin or vodka

If you are using freshly picked blackberries put them into a colander and rinse thoroughly under cold running water. Remove any stalks or leaves

Tip the blackberries into a large bowl and pour in the wine. Use a potato masher or large spoon to crush the blackberries into the wine. Cover with a tea towel and leave in a cool place for two days.

Put a sieve over another large bowl and pour the mixture into the sieve. Repeat with a clean sieve.

Pour the resulting liquid into a large pan and add the sugar. Simmer over a low heat, stirring all the while, until the sugar has dissolved completely. Keep simmering for a further 5 minutes.

Leave the mixture to cool then stir in the gin or vodka. Pour into a large measuring jug, it makes the bottling easier.

Sterilise sufficient bottles to accommodate the volume of liquid you have. Seal and label.

Websites

If you are not fortunate enough to live somewhere as ethnically diverse as East Oxford with all its small shops, you can get the ingredients I use in other places.

Flours

Many health food shops stock gluten free flours such rice, gram, tapioca and maize flour, as well as xanthan gum. The big supermarkets seem only to stock the blended flours such as gluten free flour for bread, self-raising, etc. Many of them do however stock xanthan gum.

Doves Farm Foods Ltd produces rice, gram and maize flours, and xanthan gum. Their products can be bought in health food shops. Ocada apparently also stocks them. Or you can buy directly from their website: www.dovesfarm.co.uk

Bob's Red Mill is an American employee owned company but does have a UK online shop. They stock gram and tapioca flour: www.bobsredmilluk.com

Shipton Mill now stocks a wide range of gluten free flours, including all the ones used in this book: www.shipton-mill.com

Spices

The big supermarkets now stock a wide range of herbs and spices. More difficult to source spices such as anardana (dried pomegranate seeds) and ajwain seeds can be sourced from Seasoned Pioneers www.seasonedpioneers.com

Index

CPSIA information can be obtained
at www.ICGtesting.com
Printed in the USA
LVHW071920180121
676820LV00010B/136

9 781912 850235